TH

THE VIRGIN INTERNET AUCTION GUIDE

VERSION 1.0

David Rowley

First published in Great Britain in 2000 by
Virgin Publishing Ltd
Thames Wharf Studios
Rainville Road
London W6 9HA

Version 1.0 – October 2000

A catalogue record for this book is available from the British Library.

ISBN 0 7535 0505 3

Printed by Omnia Books Limited, Glasgow

//BIDDING FOR A BARGAIN

Not so long ago it seemed that Internet auctions were just another weird US news story. A year or two later and they've caught on big in the UK too. Judging by the growth projections of the UK's biggest sites, QXL and eBay UK, the numbers taking part in Internet auctions look set to double in both 2000 and 2001.

Despite all this popularity, it is still natural to be a little hesitant when taking part in your first ever Internet auction. To help you overcome this, the first chapter of this book gives you a guided tour of what you can and cannot expect.

When you do then take part, it can still all look like you have entered some exclusive club, which you will be laughed out of, for not knowing the rules. Fear not though, as the following chapters will give you all the knowledge of an experienced Internet auction user. You will find out how to beat the competition to win auctions and how to ensure your goods are not left unsold at the end of your own auction. You will also get some advice on how to avoid common pitfalls, particularly how to recognise the bad deals and the rip-offs.

The second half of the book is a guide to the best auction sites on the Internet. As anyone who has surfed the Net knows, there's a lot of rubbish out there, so we've made every effort to filter this out first. We do not expect you to want to use all of these 400 sites, but a good many of them at least make a fascinating browse. Take a look also at top-ten trivia lists of the good, the bad and the amazing facts about Internet auctions.

David Rowley, who compiled this guide, has written about new consumer trends for *Time Out* magazine, Time Out Guidebooks, the *Independent*, *Midweek* and the *Internet Cool Guide*. His favourite auction site is eBay UK where he goes under the username 'gold-green'.

Contact us

The Internet is evolving so fast that, even though this book was correct at the time of going to press, there could be a few dud addresses or omissions. If you have any problems with anything in this book, send us an email at **response@virgin-pub.co.uk**. We'll make sure it's dealt with in the next edition.

//CONTENTS

1//AUCTIONS ON THE INTERNET

Imagine a car boot sale without the wind and rain in a field or the gloom of a car park. Imagine putting an ad in your local paper without the several days' wait to see it published and without the restriction on words used or the absence of a photo. And remember the fact that everyone in the world who has access to the web can see your online advert.

For those new to online auctions, the word 'auction' with its popular image of fine art sold to the very rich in grand rooms in Mayfair can be misleading. What they usually represent is really just a very sophisticated online classified noticeboard. Such adverts know no boundaries to class, or taste for that matter. The prices of goods bought and sold regularly range from one to one million, pounds or dollars.

//REASONS FOR USING ONLINE AUCTIONS

Online auctions are one of the Internet's great innovations. While much of the Net offers a poor man's version of events that happen in the real world, online auctions are, for most people, superior to anything that went before. Their appeal lies in their quick access to vast sources of adverts, the ease with which you can start and complete transactions and that extra spicing on top of uncertainty and excitement.

Among the best of many online auction features are the feedback ratings: the more successful trades you complete, the higher your ratings go up; the higher your ratings, the more respect you earn as a dealer and, in a snowball effect, the greater should be the number and size of your auctions. There is no such reward for someone who sells off their surplus junk in their local paper.

The feedback ratings are motivational and make auction users loyal and devoted. Not surprisingly, auction houses are among the few Internet sites that actually make profits.

How the seller benefits

Anyone who has come away from their local second-hand emporium feeling cheated and robbed should now start singing 'Oh Happy Day'. No more will you have to do battle with the terminally miserable owners of such poky caverns. The seller enters an online auction from a position of unassailable strength. Crucially, you get to set your own price from which you cannot be haggled down. In fact, simply getting at least two potential buyers making bids on your auction insures that your sale price will be higher than this minimum price.

Sellers at any decent-sized online auction site are also presenting themselves to a greater range of buyers than they would in their local papers or car boot sales.

Finally, for the seller, the online market is a dynamic and enthusiastic one. Items of junk around your house, which you would never consider advertising in your local paper, will find a market at online auctions if priced correctly. One of the reasons is that people often enjoy the process of 'winning' online auctions just as much as the process of actually acquiring something they need.

How the buyer benefits

Rummaging around for bargains is one of those archaic practices that we like to portray as fun. More often than not, though, it is tiresome and fruitless. Anyone who has had a long search for a deleted CD, an out-of-print book, or a discontinued toy will know this. You can search your local specialist shops and consult the specialist magazines time and time again for years. Chances are you will give up. The beauty of online auctions is that all their items are logged by a computer and can be retrieved by doing a few simple searches. There is a good chance that, somewhere out there, the item you seek is in an online auction.

The buyer, too, often benefits from lower prices at online auctions. The sheer size of the best online auctions means not only that sellers can reach higher prices than in local markets, but also that buyers are exposed to a greater number of sellers and therefore a greater variety of price and the likelihood of lower prices. Bargains are to be had too; not all sellers who come to online auctions appreciate the full value of what they are selling. Most sellers do not have the years of experience that retailers have; they will often overvalue their items and sometimes undervalue them.

Finally, for the buyer, the online auction, by virtue of its size, provides the most unconventional and unusual market around. There is stuff at online auctions that you will not find anywhere else. Indeed a US site (**www.e-wanted.com**) was started for this very purpose, selling spare parts for discontinued products that manufacturers and retailers could no longer be bothered to offer support for.

//FIRST STEPS

Whether you want to buy or to sell at online auctions, your first step before participating is to register with a site. Take note of the following requirements:

1   You must be 18. Below this age you are unable to sign a legally binding contract. Registering at nearly all online auctions involves agreeing to a set of site rules that are presented as a legally binding contract, which you must

sign before you can use the site. The main rule in such contracts is that you will honour all the transactions you enter into on the site.

2   You will need an email address for all communication with the online auction site and for the crucial registration page. (If you do not have an address you can quickly register for one at either www.yahoo.co.uk or www.hotmail.com.)

3   For some sites, such as Yahoo Auctions and QXL, you will need a credit card to register. This is often just an added check to see that you are aged 18 or over and that you are, for the time being, credit worthy.

Take time to think of a good nickname

On registering, you will be asked for your name, address and telephone number and, more importantly, you will also be asked to create your own username. Most common names went years ago and if you insist on being called Dave or Helen, you will have to settle for a number after it, like Dave359 or Helen22, which, strange as it may seem, some people do.

Be warned: at sites such as eBay, which has eight million users, even names you might have thought totally original have gone. Judging by some of the daft names people use, many did not come to this part of the registration process prepared. You are at liberty to change your username at a later date, though there will be a strong disincentive to do this because it will mean losing all your feedback ratings (see below).

Good usernames might reflect your location, your personality or, for the serious auctioneers, your chosen type of auction category. However, be aware that, while cheeky names like Danglebottom or Gonzobrain are common, the site will ban anything deemed truly offensive.

> eBay's top seller, who has completed over 10,000 successful deals, goes by the name parrothead88.

//TAKING PART

Most guides recommend newcomers to make their first deal as a buyer, as it requires less experience. The buyer only has to place a bid and send a cheque. Also, once this deal goes through successfully, it should lead to your first feedback point, which will make life easier when you come to do your first sale. Placing a bid, though, is not a decision to be taken lightly because, by the terms of the site's rules (which you automatically signed up to when you registered), if your bid is highest you have agreed to a legally binding contract to buy that item.

For the bidder the next stage is to check up on the auction, probably on a daily basis (auctions usually last for seven days), to see if your bid stays the highest. If by the end of the auction you have kept the highest bid, you will be sent confirmation of this by the auction site (as will the seller). On the confirmation notice will be the email address of the seller, who you will need to contact to exchange addresses so that you can send the money. On receipt of your money, the seller will send the item to you. Simple.

As a newcomer to a site, you will notice that when you place your first bid you will probably have a zero by your name. This indicates to other auction users that you have not yet completed a deal on that site. At eBay, you will also get an annoying symbol of a pair of shades next to your username. This is a drag, but everybody has been there once and at present, with the high growth in people joining online auction sites, newcomers are outnumbering the old-timers.

Once you have seen how the process of buying works, you will no doubt be tempted to create your own auction that will avail you of the opportunity to offload that surplus Beanie Baby, Dire Straits CD, Spice Girls video, Sony Walkman, bottle of Château-Lafite 1982, diamond necklace or whatever. One of the wonders of online auctions is that items that have lost their allure for you may become prized possessions for others.

Auction addiction – beware

To some, auctions will become a way of life, a daily activity that will make you wonder how you ever existed without them before. A week without posting an auction will seem like a week wasted and your life will be spent combing cupboards, garages and attics for bargains to sell off. For some sellers it will become a business, a regular alternative income. Indeed, in some cases, especially where this activity is linked to a conventional business, it can become a main source of income.

The fun of online auctions

For the seller the greatest phrase in the world of online auctions is 'bidding war'. As a seller you set a minimum price and hope it sells for a little higher than this, though you can often be in for a terrific surprise when competing buyers occasionally push the final price beyond your greatest expectations. It's a thrill you will want to repeat again and again.

For some, the competitive nature of buying at online auctions is a bore; however, for most, it adds an addictive element of risk, uncertainty and possible glory at the end of it. It is common auction etiquette for the seller to 'congratulate' the buyer on 'winning' their auction when it closes. Has that ever happened to you in a shop?

Talking of shops, have you ever wondered what it must be like to own one but never had the time to actually find out? Online auctions allow us to play at being shopkeepers on a strictly hobby basis with the minimum of effort and outlay. You can effectively become an antiques dealer or a record and CD shop overnight. You will also become a part-time advertising copywriter and marketing expert.

But I'll get ripped off, won't I?
It is quite natural to have a fear of being scammed when you enter a deal on an online auction. After all, your first contact with the seller is through their username – and probably a daft one at that.

Your chances of being ripped off, though, are probably the same as they would be while shopping in any high street in the country. If people were forever paying for goods they never received from online auctions then the auction sites would soon go out of business. The difference between a high-street shop and an online auction is that you will be an expert at spotting bad value or questionable items in high-street shops, but at an online auction you will not have learnt these rules yet. There are some pointers along these lines in Chapter 4.

//THE FEEDBACK SYSTEM EXPLAINED

In the early days of eBay they quickly realised that trade was being held back on their site by people's hesitancy to deal with complete strangers. In response they created a system to let users know who were the most reliable and trustworthy traders. After each successful transaction, the buyer and seller involved were given the opportunity of leaving a comment on the site, describing how the transaction went. Each positive comment would earn a trader a point, which was displayed next to the trader's username whenever they placed a bid or put up an advert on the site. Pretty soon, regular eBay users were accruing large points totals, or feedback ratings as they became known. The sellers with the high ratings found they had a snowball effect on trade, their sales increasing in proportion to how high their ratings were.

The feedback ratings can, of course, work in the opposite way. People who do not fulfil their legal obligation to their deals, by not buying an item they had bid on or by receiving money from a buyer but not sending the goods, are given a negative rating. These negative ratings generally provide a warning to other users that this person poses a risk if you trade with them. Ultimately, once a member's rating drops too low, they are booted off the site. At eBay this will happen when someone reaches a rating of -4, whereas at most other sites it is a -3 rating.

Most people love the idea of feedback ratings; the thought of getting those extra points makes people sell for less and pay for more. Capitalising on this, eBay award attractive stars for different levels of feedback ratings: 10 positive feedbacks equals a yellow or gold star; 100 positive feedbacks earns a blue star; 500 a purple star and 1,000 a red star. Humiliatingly, new users to eBay are given a symbol next to their name, which looks like a pair of rather ghastly red sunglasses. The company insists this symbol is not a warning, but to most experienced users it is.

No other site has such a complex feedback system, although arguably after around 100 positive feedbacks the benefits start to become less important. Amazon Auctions runs a very different system whereby you are awarded a star rating of 1–5 based on the quality of the feedback you receive, rather than on the quantity. However, feedback is not just about the points. With each feedback comes a message from the person you traded with, describing how the deal went. When awarded for deals that went well, these comments can often be bland statements of approval. They are at their most useful when describing deals that went wrong.

The feedback ratings have become so successful that any site that takes itself seriously will now have them. The only exceptions are merchant sites, where the company is the sole seller and, not surprisingly, it does not want to have negative comments about the company on its own site.

Using the feedback ratings

A high feedback rating is not always a guarantee of a safe, reliable trader. Someone with a rating of 30 may, on the surface, appear to have completed 30 successful deals. A careful trader, however, will always look behind this figure. What it could mean is that the person in question has completed 40 successful deals but has received 10 negative feedbacks from deals they did not honour. Anyone with such a regular pattern of conflicts among their feedback ratings should be treated with great caution. Too many neutral comments should be a warning sign too. At most sites, to access such feedback comments you simply click directly on to the feedback number by a trader's name.

Feedback comments can also tell you more by the way they are written. Clipped, unenthusiastic praise could mean that a user completed their deal but was problematic to deal with. Then again, how much you can read into many positive feedbacks is often undermined by the formulaic comments many leave: the habit of classing a deal as A++++ or unquantifiable comments such as 'An asset to eBay' are so common that they become near-worthless.

Be warned though: however honest, reliable and speedy you are as an auction user, being on the receiving end of some negative feedback seems unavoidable. Some people enjoy complaining. That's life. People who have been justly awarded a negative feedback by you may also retaliate and give you a similar feedback out of spite. However, the way a negative message is written often says more about the person who wrote it than it does about the person who received it. There could be a silver lining here though: if a user is truly no good, then sooner or later they will be booted off the site. Once this happens, all feedback they have awarded while using the site will be neutralised, including all positives and negatives.

As a newcomer to online auctions, life may be a little hard with a zero rating and you may face the prejudices of those who have been using the site for longer. Good auction etiquette says that we were all zero-rated once and we should treat everybody equally. However, for an experienced trader, a newcomer is someone who poses extra problems in that they will not be familiar with the transaction stage. Such deals may require extra time and patience. You will no doubt be in the same position at a later stage and may come to dread dealing with those with low or zero ratings. As a seller a deal with a newcomer may take longer, though as a buyer it is good practice to avoid purchasing expensive items from those with low feedback ratings.

Finally: if you are ever in need of cheering up, browse around for people with negative feedback and read the comments. People tend to be a lot more to the point when they are angry and such feedback can provide a riveting read.

Leaving feedback

You are encouraged to leave feedback after every transaction. The feedback system, however, is not compulsory and occasionally you may leave someone glowing feedback and they will not bother to reply. Some people may be lazy or disinterested in leaving feedback. The most you can do is be proactive about encouraging feedback by stating in your end-of-deal emails to fellow traders that all successful transactions result in positive feedback.

When you come to write your first feedback comment, you may be stumped as to exactly what to write. To work this out, ask yourself if the other person contacted you quickly. Did they accept your payment terms without loads of queries? Were they polite? Did the cheque arrive quickly? Did they pack your purchase responsibly? Refer to any of the above if they particularly impressed you.

//TERMS AND CONDITIONS

When you register at an online auction site, at the bottom of the form, before you submit your details, there will usually be a sentence explaining that by clicking the submit button you are automatically agreeing to the site's terms and conditions.

A site's terms and conditions are usually long, dull legal documents that you will be sorely tempted to ignore. If you do this and feel a pang of conscience, here in a simplified form is what most terms and conditions for consumer-to-consumer auctions say:

1 If you are under 18, you cannot sign a legal agreement or commit to a binding business deal; come back when you are older.

2 Whether you are bidding on an item or you are selling it, once the auction has ended and there is a bidder in

place, both of you are legally obliged to make the deal go through.

3   If you get ripped off in an auction transaction it is not our fault. So do not even think of suing us, because you can't.

4   We, as the auction site, are under no obligation to help out with any ugly buyer–seller disputes.

5   Your adverts must be honest and must not contain computer viruses.

6   If we find out about you selling anything stolen, dodgy or unpleasant (e.g. guns, porno, drugs, stolen property, manuals on how to make bombs, pirated software, CDs or videos), we will stop the auction.

7   If you are a nutcase and abuse other members with offensive language, we will boot you off our site forever.

8   If we find out that you boosted the price of your auction by shilling (using a false identity to bid for your own items), we will boot you off our site forever.

9   If our server crashes and disrupts your auction adversely, you cannot sue us.

10 In case you skipped the opening points, if you get ripped off remember that it is not our fault, so do not sue us.

Note that the terms and conditions for merchant auctions will differ. As they are the ones doing the selling, they should also be the ones sorting out any disputes.

//A BRIEF HISTORY OF E-COMMERCE AND COMMUNITY

The eBay success story

The most important date in the history of online auctions is 5 September 1995. This was the start date for Echo Bay Web Auction or Auctionweb.com, now better and more simply known as eBay.

The company's path from being a one-man operation to becoming the billion-dollar business it is today is often spun as a simple stroke of luck, though Internet success stories are never quite as easy as that. Pierre Omidyar, the man who dreamed up eBay, was in 1995 already working as a software engineer in Silicon Valley, California, with a special interest in developing shopping sites. His imagination was sparked by his fiancée Linda's complaint about her inability to collect Pez sweet dispensers, colourful plastic tubes with a flip-back head that reveals a rectangular tablet. Linda had contact with those who traded in Pez in the San Francisco Bay area but was finding that market too limited.

Pierre decided to create a solution on the Internet. More than just a simple contact forum of the style that already existed, he created software that would allow the placing of adverts by potential sellers and the placing of competing bids by potential buyers. The site was an instant hit and its low overheads meant that eBay, like many auction sites to follow, was quickly profitable.

eBay has always managed to stay one step ahead of its competitors, who entered the market with better funding and contacts. The reasons are that, firstly, it has constantly updated and improved its software, innovating most of the features of online auctions that are commonplace today (e.g. feedback ratings); to this day it is the most technically advanced auction site on the Net. Secondly, such superior software has brought eBay the benefit of large word-of-mouth (or mouse) recommendations from its users. For this reason it has never had to rely on big advertising campaigns.

The company is already thinking ahead by establishing a network of sites all over the world. Unlike QXL, which has concentrated on expanding in Europe, eBay has concentrated on English-language countries across the globe, opening sites in Australia, New Zealand, Canada and the UK (October 1999) as well as branching out into the lucrative markets of Japan and Germany.

Some big-number facts and rumours about eBay

- It is said that 70% of all online auctions take place at eBay.

- By 1997 eBay was growing at 30,000 users a week.

- When eBay first started selling stock, in September 1998, the price per share was $18 (£12) – within two months it was selling at over $230 (£152) per share.

- In 1999 it was reported that where eBay was doing over $8 million (£5.3 million) worth of deals a day on the Net, Yahoo was doing $480,000 (£317,000) and Amazon $300,000 (£200,000).

- In the first quarter of 2000, eBay generated gross merchandise sales of $1.2 billion (£0.8 billion) – a 33% increase over the gross merchandise sales of $901 million (£600,000) for the last quarter of 1999.

- In 1999 eBay was reported as trying to buy the traditional auction house of Sotheby's; instead it settled for the US auction house of Butterfields.

- At the beginning of 2000 there were more than 4.5 million items for auction, with over 400,000 new items added each day in more than 4,000 categories.

- In mid-2000 there were 15.8 million registered individuals.

- One million items are sold every day and almost half a million new items are listed every day.

- eBay reputedly boasts the highest sales completion record of all sites, with a success rate of between 50 and 75%. Of those selling through eBay, 20% make it a business.

- In 2000 eBay was voted the eighth best site on the Internet.

Catching up – the websites that have followed eBay

Other entrepreneurs spotted eBay's quick success and in 1996 many new auction sites were created. The most successful realised that, although eBay had established itself as a site where ordinary consumers met up to trade in rare collectible items, it was by no means a specialist in the other markets, particularly computers. One of the first companies to make its mark as an auction site specialising in computer hardware and software was Haggle (**www.haggle.com**). Following on its heels were the manufacturers and retailers of computers, who started up sites to sell off their surplus stock in low-priced auctions. The largest of these sites to this day is Egghead (**www.egghead.com**).

There are now hundreds of auction sites run as going concerns in the USA. Undoubtedly the country's love of unfettered capitalism has played a part in their success. Those who buy through auction sites are raised from the level of passive consumers into wheeler-dealer traders seeking the going market price. There has been some talk in the USA that the auction format is becoming so popular that the idea of paying a fixed price for anything will become outdated. This is naïve, as although the auction format is a fun alternative to ordinary shopping, on the whole it is more time-consuming.

The UK enters the market

The first site to try to replicate eBay in the UK was QXL, in September 1997. QXL prospered for some time, largely due to the delay in eBay establishing itself in the UK. Even though eBay UK looks set to eclipse it, QXL has benefited from an enormous amount of publicity and, in doing so, has established itself as the number one site in the collective consciousness of the British public, if not in numbers.

With funds derived from its stock-market flotation, QXL has pursued a policy of expanding into the virgin European auction market. It famously made a loss of £31 million to the year ending March 2000, despite an initially soaring share price. However, in April 2000 the number of members had doubled from the previous December. In total, including its European sites, it had 600,000 members at the end of April 2000.

The future

The gold rush of new online auction sites looks to be coming to an end. The next battle is one of survival as the big companies fight to gain the greatest number of members and listings.

There are already many auction sites on the Net with wonderful software and catchy names, but next to no auctions. You may well find that, by the time you look up some of the companies listed in this directory, some have already given up the fight.

//TYPES OF ONLINE AUCTIONS

Standard online auction

The most common online auction is the consumer-to-consumer auction, often known as C2C. Found at the auction sites of eBay, Yahoo and QXL, it typically features a second-hand item being sold to the highest bidder over a seven- or fourteen- day period. This is sometimes known as an English auction in the USA.

Merchant auctions and surplus auctions

Merchant auctions or business-to-consumer auctions (B2C) are a grand name for what are more often than not auctions of surplus goods. Wholesalers, retailers and manufacturers with excess or discontinued stock and seconds, returns, shop-soiled or graded stock have found that auctions are a great way to turn such dead weight into cash.

Often, as there will be more than one of each item on offer, these auctions are effectively Dutch auctions (see below). Basically, for the buyer this translates as a very good chance of winning. Although somewhat lacking the excitement of standard auctions, merchant auctions have the advantages of being able to pay by credit card, quick professional shipping and a guarantee for whatever you have bought, which allows you to return the item painlessly if there is anything at fault.

Local auctions

Sofas, armchairs, beds, greenhouses, cars and so on are all too large to make it worthwhile shipping them very far. In response, many auction sites in the USA have set up to cater for individual cities (e.g. **www.auctionsorlando.com** and the *Los Angeles Times* auction at **www.laauctions.com**). In the UK, local auctions are currently limited to such sites as Loot, which allow you to search by area. In the same way that Loot has built upon its classified ads base to start its auctions, local papers in your area might decide to get in on this act. In the USA, eBay can be searched by US state and this may well be a development in the future with eBay UK.

Dutch auctions

The most confusing of auction formats, a Dutch auction allows several winners for several items. A good example of how this auction works is where a company may have surplus stock, for example, ten Epson printers. Rather than sell them in individual auctions, the company auctions them together as a single lot. Buyers looking to buy a single printer and those looking to buy more than one are both allowed to bid. If, though, as often happens, there are ten bidders who all want a single printer then they will all win.

This format gets confusing when you take price into account. Dutch auction rules mean that the lowest price put forward by any of the bidders becomes the final price paid by all (in this case) ten bidders. Further rules state that where there are more than ten bidders, the person with the lowest bid loses out. Also, where there are excess bidders who all share the same low bid, the earlier bids gain precedence or those with the higher-quantity bids win. And, finally, there are no automatic bids allowed (see page 25).

In the USA there is a variation on the Dutch auction, known as the Yankee auction or American auction, where each winner pays the price they bid at and not that of the lowest bidder.

Promotional auctions

These are a mixed blessing. Often a company will sell a new item at a ridiculously low price on a high-profile auction site. In doing so they will gain some free media attention and log their product into the minds of the people using the site. Typically, such an auction might be for a brand-new car with a starting bid of £1 (or $1).

Tempting as these auctions are, they are usually so popular and high profile that whatever is for sale often goes for only a little less than what it would cost new. Such auctions can be found at **www.fsauctions.co.uk**, **www.bezign.com** and **www.firedup.com**.

Declining auction

A great gimmick, the declining auction has not at the time of writing been tried out in the UK, but is to be found at US sites such as **www.reverseauction.com**. Simply, this works by instead of starting an auction at its minimum price, you start it at a high or maximum price. Over the course of the auction a computer deducts a cent at a time from the price – for expensive items such as cars you can watch the value drop by the second. A buyer can wait until the item has reached a price they think is reasonable before bidding. The first bid automatically wins the item. The bidder of course knows that the longer they wait, the higher the chance that someone may bid before them.

Real-time auctions

This rather grand phrase is the term that Internet users give to old-fashioned auctions that have a gavel-wielding person on a raised platform taking bids from a crowd of people. They are so named as they take place in the 'real' world, not because they are any more valid than auctions held on the Net. Many of these traditional auctions have dragged themselves warily on to the net by allowing email bids for their auctions. These bids will sometimes be made in advance of the auction, while others will allow you to bid live over the few minutes that the auction takes place. Log on too late here and you can miss the whole auction. Such auctions can be found at www.ibidlive.com and www.auctionchannel.com.

Reverse auctions

This is really just a variation on 'wanted ads'; at a reverse auction it is the buyer who places the advert and the sellers who have to place competitively priced bids. Top reverse auctions are at www.ewanted.com and www.reversebids.co.uk.

Private auctions

These auctions are rare but allow anonymity to bidders who may not want people to know they are bidding on an item. This could be for items of great expense or for embarrassing items such as pornography.

2//UNDER THE HAMMER –
A BUYER'S GUIDE

Before bidding on anything in an online auction always take into account the following 'golden' rules:

1   When you enter a bid, and in the event of you winning the auction, by the terms and conditions of the site you will have entered into a binding legal agreement to buy that item. Even if you are not legally pursued for backing out of a deal, you are opening yourself up to negative feedback.

2   Read the item descriptions carefully before you bid.

3   Ask the seller questions before you bid, not after.

4   Always take into account how much the shipping costs will add to the price of an item. If this is not shown, email the seller and ask for details. Be aware that shipping insurance, packaging, money order and escrow costs can all add to the price too.

5   Contact the seller within three days of the auction's close or risk a negative feedback or the possibility that they may decide instead to deal with the second-highest bidder.

//SEARCHING

When first using an online auction it is natural to want to have a browse around to get a feel for what is on offer. Once you are past this stage though, browsing will become tiresome and a waste of time. If you know exactly what you want, it is far easier to use the search function or search box, found on the home page of any decent online auction site.

Search boxes come with their own set of rules that vary from site to site. If you are using eBay and seeking *The Sound of Music* on CD, simply typing in Sound of Music will produce a long list of search results of auctions with any of these three words in their title. To narrow this down put speech marks around the words, i.e. 'Sound of Music'. To narrow it down further you might want to write 'Sound of Music' +CD. This will capture all listings with the exact phrase 'Sound of Music' in them and with CD in the title. Similarly, if the CD listings happen to be the largest search result and this is not what you are looking for, you can filter out such results by typing 'Sound Of Music' -CD. QXL has a similar search system, the exact rules for which are found on the link next to its search box and marked 'advanced search'.

eBay searches are the most advanced of all online auction sites. They will also let you search by price range, the seller's country of location, by seller username and, if you should wish, by recently completed auctions.

An advanced search tip

Many items may either be spelled incorrectly or have various valid spellings; for example, a search on Beanie Baby will produce a different set of results to Beanie Babies. Also, if you are searching by category alone, be aware that some items can qualify for another category too. For example, a book on Princess Diana could be found under memorabilia (this is where most items about her are to be found) or it could be found under books. Similarly, items may be posted to a completely wrong category. The general rule here is that if your exact search has not revealed what you are seeking, it may be worth ploughing through the results of a more inexact one that covers most of the site.

Searching for bargains Bargains are best snapped up at the end of the auction rather than at the beginning. Both eBay and Yahoo at present have pre-programmed searches for items that are due to finish either within the next hour or within one day. At eBay there is also a special bargain page, which can be found on its site map.

Item alerts Cannot find what you are looking for? You need not log on every day to repeat your search because there are many services at online auctions that will do this for you automatically. eBay's Personal Shopper page allows you to list up to three items. When one of these is listed at eBay, you will get an email informing you of this. Most other sites have similar functions, while some auction help sites such as **www.itrack.com** offer a service that searches across multiple sites.

//BEFORE YOU BID

Assessing an advert We all tend to envisage things as we would like them to be, instead of what they are in reality. Cast a suspicious eye on descriptions about condition in an advert; 'very good condition' may mean 'almost perfect' in your mind, but to the seller it could mean 'good condition, considering how much wear it's had'.

Another good rule is to match the photo accompanying an advert with its description – are they the same? Suspicions about description might be allayed if you do a search on the seller's other auctions (this is possible at eBay). If the seller has many similar adverts then they probably know what they are talking about; if not, approach the item with suspicion.

Assessing the price If you are unsure of the going price for an item you are about to bid on, you can gain an idea of its market value by looking at the prices gained at closed auctions. This search is available at the top of each category page at eBay and Yahoo.

Questions to ask a seller during the auction Although site rules stipulate that descriptions should be honest, it is a natural instinct of a seller to skimp on the truth when it comes to flaws, faults and scratches. If you suspect that something might be flawed, or information is missing, write to the seller and ask very specific questions; for example, if an item is of great value, it is not unusual to ask to see more photos.

Common questions also concern the methods of payment and shipping. It is very frustrating for a seller to have to answer questions of such a nature after the auction. If you have a payment or shipping request that differs from what is stated in the description then you should sort this out before the auction ends, and preferably before you bid.

//BIDDING STRATEGIES

Bid early or late? There are two schools of thought on this. One says that if you join an auction early and immediately bid the maximum amount you are prepared to pay then you will scare off interest from other bidders, who might otherwise generate a bidding war. The downside to this is that your bid might encourage the curiosity of people eager to know what attracted your attention.

The more popular late-bidding school of thought argues that if you bid late you reduce to a minimum the chance of a bidding war. A bid like this in the last few minutes of an auction is known as sniping (see below).

Sniping Sniping is a dirty word in some auction circles; others, though, see it as a perfectly legitimate practice. The process of only declaring your interest in an auction at the very last minute can lull others who have already bid into a false sense of security. When the original bidders find that they have lost an auction in which they had the highest bid for several days, many get understandably bitter. To counter such sniping, Yahoo Auctions will extend any auction that has received any last-minute bids by five minutes. At eBay and QXL, though, there is no such device and it is here where most sniping takes place.

If you see an item on auction that absolutely has to be yours but it has already received another bid, the recommended effective guide to sniping is as follows. In the final minutes of the auction, open up the bidding page and type out the details of your bid. Next, open up the auction site a second time in another window, to show the main page for the item you desire. As the seconds tick by, keep pressing the reload button on the top tool bar of your screen, to keep a check on the price. If the price goes up then amend your bidding page accordingly. Wait until the final ten seconds of the auction before submitting your bidding page with the winning bid. Generally, bids take up to ten seconds to process; if you leave your bid any later, it may be too late.

Automatic bidding If you find that over the course of an auction someone is, or several people are, consistently topping your bids then, to save time, you would be well advised to use the site's automatic bidding system, or autobid as it is commonly known. This works by letting you state the absolute maximum you would be comfortable paying (e.g. \$20). It then lets you start your bidding at a much lower price (e.g. \$10). To follow the example, as soon as someone else bids $11, the autobid mechanism will raise your bid to $12. The autobid will go on bidding on your behalf, as long as no one bids higher than $20. Even if you are outbid, the autobid will send you an email telling you about this. It is important to note that if no one else bids on this auction then you will not be forced into paying your maximum bid. Your original bid becomes the final price and the seller need be none the wiser.

To confuse matters, the autobid device goes by different names at different sites. At eBay it is called 'Proxy Bid'; elsewhere it is called 'Bid For Me', 'Bid Assist', 'Robo Bid' and the long-winded 'Maximum Proxy Bid Agent'. The most common name among the sites in this guide is Autobid, which says exactly what it is, an automatic bid.

//TIPS DURING THE AUCTION

Backing out of a bid Sellers hate it when bidders back out of a bid during an auction, but in some instances it is permissible. Although you are not allowed to pull out of an auction that has ended, while it is still live you can email a seller and ask them to cancel your bid. This might happen if, by accident, you have entered the wrong amount on the bid form and wish to re-enter a different bid.

Also, if you have second thoughts about an auction and just want to pull out, you may again ask the seller to cancel your bid. The seller, though, is well within their rights to give you negative feedback for such a practice. Indeed, do it too often and the site will cancel your registration.

The only acceptable times you are allowed to withdraw a bid are, firstly, when a seller's feedback rating falls below zero during the auction and, secondly, when they do not reply to one of your emailed questions or when they change the description or photo midway through an auction.

A timesaving tip After you have placed your bid you will no doubt want to check up on the state of bidding each day. To save yourself time logging on to a site and finding your appropriate page each time, create a direct link to that auction page on your desktop. You can do this by right clicking on the page with your mouse and then choosing the 'Create a shortcut' option.

Returning shoddy goods If an item plainly does not match the description it had on the auction site, it is commonly accepted by experienced sellers that you may send the item back and ask for your money back. Before you do this email them, politely describe your problem and state that you would like to return the item for a full refund. Thank the seller in advance, send back the item and wait for the cheque to arrive.

Scam alert – shilling Shilling is a scam perpetrated by sellers who try to encourage a bidding war, and therefore a higher sale price, by bidding on their own items. The seller does this by setting up a second identity at the auction site to place 'competing' (or shill) bids. In some instances they may get an accomplice to do this for them.

In the spring of 2000, a thirty-member shilling ring was discovered at eBay after an investigation by a US newspaper. All were strongly suspected of bidding up the price of each other's auctions and eBay ended up suspending fifteen members of the ring for one month. There was some indignation by regular users that eBay did not take a tougher stance. Presumably eBay lacked conclusive proof, although all offenders were warned that a second offence would see them banned for life. If you have any suspicions about shilling you should report it immediately to the site.

//BUYING FROM THE USA

As most of what sells at online auctions is from the USA, it does not make sense to cut yourself off from this choice. Buying from the USA, though, is not something that should be treated lightly and should only be approached by someone who has already had experience of buying from within the UK first.

Bear in mind too that not everything on sale in the USA is available for export. In fact, most auctions are weighted against selling internationally by making the 'I will not ship internationally' a default setting on the 'create an auction' entry form. Always check whether someone is prepared to ship abroad before you buy.

The American view on international buyers

Selling internationally is a hot topic among US auction users; some are in favour and others are dead against. A long-running debate on this subject can be found at **www.auctionwatch.com**'s forum pages.

Many of those who do not wish to ship abroad have had bad experiences in the past and see it as too problematic. Firstly, a US seller has to fill out a customs form, which may incur the buyer extra charges they were not expecting and thus complicate the payment process. Many also resent being asked by buyers to lie about the package's contents so as to escape customs duties – the responsibility for such action lies entirely with the sender. Secondly, a low-cost mailing may take an eternity to reach its destination, during which time the seller may have to field frantic email messages from the unhappy buyer suspecting a scam and threatening negative feedback. The willingness of US sellers to ship abroad is also not helped by many US online auction guidelines that warn 'There are risks dealing with foreign nationals, underage persons or people acting under false pretences'!

On occasions, if a US seller has not ticked the 'I will ship internationally' box, they can be persuaded into doing so – especially if their item has no bids on it. It could be the case that they had a bad experience with a particular country and they are maybe better disposed to dealing with someone from the UK, someone who for a start speaks their own language. The rule here is that if a seller has not ticked the 'I will ship internationally' box, you must always make an enquiry by email first before you even think of bidding. Having a high feedback rating might be persuasive, as would the promise of a quick and easy payment route.

Fortunately there are many US sellers who welcome bids from abroad, largely as this increases their chance of making a sale. Sometimes US sellers recognise too that foreign bidders are prepared to pay more than an American for an item they could not find in their own country. Some sellers also just enjoy the contacts it makes them overseas.

Bearing all this in mind, if a US seller is prepared to ship abroad, treat them with extra respect.

Questions to ask yourself before buying from the USA

1   Can it be bought cheaper in the UK?

2   Will the cost of the shipping make it worthwhile?

3   If it is an electrical item, will it work on UK plugs?

4   Will it have a valid guarantee for the UK?

Prices If you want to know exactly what you will be paying in dollars, the Bloomberg Currency Convertor (**www.bloomberg.com/markets/currency/currcalc.cgi**) has a nifty device that lets you type a dollar value and then automatically converts the value into UK pounds.

Shipping Shipping from the USA may take anything from a couple of weeks, for the cheapest US mail service, to an overnight delivery if you request a Federal Express service. If you wish to work out the cost of a standard US mailing to the UK, a guide to prices is found at **www.usps.gov/business/calcs.htm**.

Time differences US auctions are held in any one of four time zones. This should not be a problem generally since most sites have a countdown in term of days, hours and minutes (e.g. auction to end in 3 days, 5 hours and 2 minutes) rather than in terms of the local time.

However, it maybe worth knowing that PST is Pacific Time, which is eight hours behind the UK, MST is Mountain Time, which is seven hours behind, CST is Central Time, which is six hours behind, and EST is Eastern Time, which is five hours behind.

Paying US sellers

Payment can be your biggest problem. International money orders from UK banks can cost up to £8 to purchase, while a US dollar cheque written out by a UK bank may still incur bank charges of up to $8 in the USA for the seller. A cheaper way may be to ask your bank to wire the money over.

For small purchases, one of the easiest, though riskiest, alternatives may be to send the actual dollars in the post. Generally this is to be advised against, but it could be an option if you are dealing with a seller you are familiar with or one who has a high feedback rating. Many of the bigger sellers on eBay may have credit card processing facilities, making it easier for international buyers to pay. One way of both quickening things up and providing security is to use an escrow service (see later).

One of the most popular methods of payment in the USA is a credit card service found at **www.paypal.com**. This enables you to use a credit card to pay the service company, which in turn sends a cheque to the seller. At present this service is not available in the UK, but PayPal are looking to open here soon. Until then, the following represent some of the easiest methods of getting payment to the USA.

First-e   **www.first-e.com**

eBay have set up links with this French bank ('Europe's first Internet bank') especially for UK members who want to trade with the USA. The system works by first registering with First-e and then transferring them the funds for your deal from your UK bank account. Next, First-e generate a cheque in the USA with an affiliated US bank and send it to your seller. For this you will be charged a competitively priced £3.10. If you are the seller, the bank can also process US dollar cheques into your account or into a UK sterling cheque sent to you five days later. The bank offers interest for money kept there and generally you are encouraged to keep the proceeds from your sales at the bank, in order to pay for your purchases.

Billpoint   **www.billpoint.com**

This credit card payment service allows UK buyers to pay US sellers on eBay by credit card, though at the time of writing not vice versa. This popular service, owned by eBay, acts as a third party in a transaction to allow buyers to pay by credit card. To use this service you should first contact your US seller, who then has to register their details on to the Billpoint site. Billpoint then send an online invoice to you as the buyer. You then fill in the invoice with your credit card details and mail it back to Billpoint, which then takes payment and passes it on to the seller, minus a charge of around 4.5%.

Ccnow   **www.ccnow**

Ccnow does a similar job to Billpoint, but charges the seller 9%. The only reason for using this service is that, unlike Billpoint, it is available across a wider range of sites.

//AUCTION SEARCH AND ITEM SEARCH SITES

If you cannot find what you are looking for at the auction site of your choice, the following sites will save you time searching elsewhere. Auction search sites work by searching across a wide range of anything between 10 and 300 auction sites on a daily basis and then storing the information for you to access. Type in a search here and you will be presented with a list of matching items over a variety of online auction sites. Click on any item and you will be taken directly to the relevant bidding page. Be aware that, while a useful guide, these search sites are rarely 100% accurate and occasionally contain auctions that have closed.

There is a question mark over the future of these search sites, as eBay claims such 'spider' sites end up slowing down the links at its site. Recently eBay won a court case stopping Biddersedge from searching its site.

The best

Auctionwatch   **www.auctionwatch.com**

A recent search here revealed access to listings of 127,000 stamps, 100,000 Beanies, 152,000 CDs and 131,000 records.

Bidfind   www.bidfind.com

The best of the auction search sites misses out what you have probably looked at already (eBay, Yahoo and Amazon) and instead searches up to 400 other sites with up to 400,000 items listed. Extras here are a list of new auction sites, auction software sites, a guide on how to host one-off auctions with your own URL, a wanted-items page and that all-important five-monthly Beanie Baby price index.

I Track   www.itrack.com

If you have grown fed up of trawling websites endlessly searching for that rare Beanie Baby, Pokémon card or long-deleted CD, then this site will do the job for you. Register on a simple form and then list up to five types of search for the site to perform. These take place at a handful of top sites including eBay, Amazon and Yahoo. Next, sit back and the site will email you when an auction turns up. For larger searches and extra services you will need to pay a $25 (about £16.50) registration fee.

The rest

Antiques Bulletin Online   www.antiquesbulletinonline.com

A short but well-chosen list of online auction sites specialising in antiques, as well as an antiques chat room, articles, wanted ads pages, news and links to dealers.

Auction Insider   www.auctioninsider.com

Some interesting but questionable analyses of the top ten auction sites. Also a newsletter and links to sites with auction software.

Auction Octopus   www.auctionoctopus.com

Item searches from top US sites including Yahoo, AltaVista, Amazon and Onsale.com; also online auction news.

Biddersedge   www.biddersedge.com

With links to over 100 sites, this is another of the top search sites, though it recently lost the right to search under eBay. If you cannot find what you are looking for here, leave details of your search and the site will email you if and when that item comes up for auction.

Bidstream   www.bidstream.com

No eBay or Yahoo but a good selection of sites to search on here.

The Hot100   www.hot100.com

This site provides irresistible, but debatable, lists of the top 100 websites on a wide range of subjects including online auctions. Strangely, it makes eBay number 2 to Yahoo Auctions and many of its links are old or not working, but this is worth a little look if you are bored.

Internet Auction List   www.internetauctionlist.com

This site produces very similar searches to that at Biddersedge. Its pages, though, are overloaded with many worthy (but rather disappointing) features, such as a guide to the best sites to sell your items, a price comparison of items at 150 online auction sites, lists of auctions by country and new auction sites on the net.

I Stores   www.i-stores.co.uk

A directory of UK websites with a good range of UK auctions.

Lifestyle.UK   www.lifestyle.co.uk

A long list of UK auctions can be found at this shopping directory.

Online.Auctions Net   www.online-auctions.net

Item searches and some rather dubious grading of top auction sites by differing attributes such as ease of use and reliability.

UKMax   www.ukmax.co.uk

One of the best general directories of UK websites.

A good general search engine

For specialist sites that deal in some obscure collectibles, your best port of call is Google.

Google   **www.google.com**

The most brilliant and popular search engine on the net. Type in the item you are looking for (e.g. fossil, rings, maps, software) followed by the words 'online auction'. If you are only interested in UK sites, type in 'UK' too.

3//UNDER THE HAMMER – A SELLER'S GUIDE

//PREPARING THE ADVERT

A bland description, a low price and a good photo will often be enough to sell an item. For those new to selling, a low-value item at a cheap price to guarantee a sale may be good introduction into the process of selling at online auctions. If, however, you are interested in making regular sales with lucrative returns, read on.

One of the most important rules of selling is to remember that people buy for both rational and emotional reasons. A good advert description contains a balance of each.

Being rational
When covering the rational side of a buyer's needs, think in terms of describing the item to someone who cannot see the photo. This might sound strange but, owing to the small element of risk involved in online dealing, people need reassuring that the description is exactly the same as the photo they see.

It pays to be honest about an item's flaws. Not mentioning them may get you more bids and a higher price, but will also give you a whole lot of worry about buyers returning the goods, demanding their money back and giving you negative feedback. A fault or scratch need not be written in a negative way. One guide recommends a description along the lines of 'a flaw that does not affect the structural integrity in any way'.

If inspiration is slow in coming, then take a look around at how other people have written theirs. Look at both what you like about their adverts and what you think leaves something to be desired and learn from it. A good starting point is the description on any advert with a high number of bids.

Give it some emotion

A miserable, stingy little description sends out a poor message, not least that this person is going to be no fun doing business with. Make the description upbeat and enthusiastic. Get the balance right though. Some go overboard by peppering their ads with exclamation marks!!! AND BIG CAPITAL LETTERS!!! Adverts like these look too good to be true and wise buyers will avoid them. Many of the clinical, old advertising clichés do work though; words like new, rare, limited, bonus, extra, plus and free are corny, but they trigger acquisitive impulses in buyers' brains.

Think about the buyer when you are writing the description. Write it in terms of the benefits it can bring to the reader. If the item is a collectible, put in something about its history, where you bought it, how long you have had it and who the previous owner was. For many collectors such tales add value to an item. People also get more emotional over limited-edition items or artistic items. If your advert can drum up enough emotion, people might be prepared to bid much higher amounts.

Writing the title

Your title, depending on how it is written, can win or lose you bids. This is because many buyers do not browse but simply do a search on an item from the home page. This is especially true for over-loaded categories like CDs, books, computer software, Pokémon and Beanie Babies. If your title is not descriptive enough or misspelled, it can lose out in such searches. If your item is being sold in a small category where people are more likely to browse, try to make the item stand out on the page. Emotional words, like rare, new, exciting and bargain will get you more hits. Some people go to even greater lengths to attract attention: !!!@@ when placed next to a title looks ridiculous but, by some strange logic, this approach seems to generate a higher amount of bids.

Further writing tips

- To save time and money online, prepare the text first on your computer and then cut and paste it to the site.

- Sellers who have had bad experiences with deadbeat bidders may want to state in their advert that 'The highest bidder to prepay within 14 days or the seller will relist'.

- If your shipping terms are low then emphasise this as a selling point.

- For a more accurate advert, check the descriptions found on a manufacturer's website.

Useful HTML for your advert

The 'create an auction' pages of online auction sites have automatically programmed HTML that allows you to print your text as you write it. Knowledge of a few HTML codes, though, can make a big impression to your advert. The following codes are commonly used.

Putting <center> </center> around a title will position it in the middle of a page; note the US spelling for this code.

Using <br> will break text to give you a new line.

Putting <b> </b> around text makes the words appear in bold.

A <hr> code creates a line to separate text. There is one of these at the top of eBay's home page.

Put <p> at the start of a paragraph and </p> at the end to separate it from other text.

Where you want to make a list of separate points use <ul> to start, followed by <li> for each separate point and </ul> to close the list.

If you would like to give a little extra individuality to your description, the following may help. The essence of consumer-to-consumer auctions is informality. Remember though, too much colour may put people off.

<h1> creates a heading in larger text than what follows </h1>

<font color = '#FF0000'> creates red text </font>

<font color='#0000FF'> creates blue text </font>

<blink> creates text that blinks </blink>

For a list of different fonts take a look at HTML Goodies (**www. htmlgoodies.com**). 'If you know nothing about HTML, this is where you start', reassures this site, which offers the easiest HTML guide on the net and generally reads like it was written by a human rather than a computer geek. Further to the above HTML codes, there is also a list of ten fonts here: click 'Master List' on the bottom left of the home page, then 'html references' and then 'text'.

Creating a website link You can use your advert description to promote your website. The following html will create a direct link: <a href= 'http://www.yoursite.co.uk'>. The main rule to remember here is that online auction sites do not take kindly to you promoting anything on your website that might compete with the service they are offering.

If you want an idea of the number of people viewing your auctions, the Honesty site (**www.honesty.com**) will provide you with free counters.

Which category? This might sound like a dumb question, but for many items there are often two or more good categories for it to go in. The category that looks to be getting the greater number of bids is probably your best bet.

Which site? eBay has more bidders than any other site and for many this is the deciding factor in placing their auctions there. However, in a bid to compete with eBay, many sites will offer free listings or lower commission fees.

Payment details

The absence of clear payment details or shipping costs in an advert might scare off bidders suspecting the worst. Work them out first and, to clarify, place these details at the end of your description. Also, if your item is worth hundreds or thousands of pounds, offer an escrow service. This gives added confidence to a buyer nervous of spending such large amounts.

Payment by cheque is common among most UK auctions, but its downside is that it can make transactions drag out for longer as you wait for it to clear. Money orders cost extra for buyers but can be quickly cashed to speed a deal along. If, as a seller, you want such speed of payment, you could offer to deduct the bank charges incurred by the buyer in purchasing the money order.

When working out your shipping costs do not forget to include packaging cost too. To clarify these shipping costs you may also want to specify which shipping method you are using.

//BANNED ITEMS

Distasteful, illegal and degrading. No self-respecting auction site wishes to be associated with these words and will pull any auction that breaches its rules on what can or cannot be sold on its site. Until auction software can be invented to stop such auctions taking place though, the top sites will have to live with a certain number of such adverts on their sites. Quite often the first a site hears of such an auction is when it appears in a newspaper story. It is interesting to note that a search on the top three four-letter words brought a zero response at eBay but yielded a quite prolific response at Yahoo Auctions.

eBay has suffered more from notorious auctions than any other site. Consequently they have one of the biggest lists of banned items among all the sites. These fall into three categories and have much in common with other auction sites.

1 Illegal – stolen or pirated goods, or banned goods such as drugs.

2 Offensive – pornography, human or animal parts, guns.

3 Inappropriate – alcohol, food, live animals, fireworks, drugs paraphernalia.

This last category might seem a little contentious since many sites sell wine; however, as eBay is well aware, many teenagers too young to use the site do get in and it does not want the bad publicity that could arise from such incidents.

Yahoo Auctions does not ban alcohol and has a much smaller list. Indeed, Yahoo Auctions has the least restrictions of almost any big auction site. A spin-off of this has been the encouraging of spoof auctions on their site: in the summer of 2000, the unfortunate 'Jake

Martin' was being auctioned by someone from Sugar Grove, Oklahoma, under the heading Stupid Person and under the category of Other Goods and Services.

Where banned items slip through the above restrictions at online auctions, beware that those selling them are hardly going to be the most trustworthy members of the site.

//SELLING STRATEGIES

Many approach online auctions with an ingrained fear of being forced into selling an item at less than they want. The beauty of online auctions is that this never need happen. You are free to set a minimum price below which no bids can be accepted.

Offer a bargain

People buy from online auctions either because they are looking for rare items or because they are looking for a bargain. If you are honest with yourself and accept that your Alba midi system is not going to become a collector's item, give it a low price. Remember too that the buyer is not getting any after-sales customer care or a year's guarantee from you. They also have the risk of buying from a complete stranger and then the shipping costs to pay on top.

In general, pricing something at half the price it would cost in a shop is a good strategy. If you think you are offering a bargain compared to current shop prices, put it in your description. Of course, setting a low price does not mean that it will sell at that price; the lower the price, the greater the chance the item will be bid up. Along these lines some suggest a strategy of pricing an item at between 10% and 20% of the price you want for it. Occasionally you may find that if an item is priced very low then a dealer snaps it up. If they think that they can sell it for a greater price then good luck to them, that is their business.

If you are still in doubt about what price you should charge, then study the prices at closed auctions. This can be done at Amazon, eBay and Yahoo. Look at the going prices for items similar to yours and work out what might be a good price.

Timing your auction

Unlike in the USA, where Internet costs are cheaper, most people in the UK log on in the evening or at the weekend. So, ideally plan to close your UK auction somewhere between Saturday afternoon and Sunday afternoon. (It is also said that parents often buy for their children at weekends, when they all sit at the computer to bid together).

Another good policy is to end your auction at the start of a month. Most people tend to get paid at the end of the month and are therefore a little more happy-go-lucky with their money at this time. As a general rule, try to think about the audience you are selling to and when they are most likely to be using the Net.

While most auctions are seven days long, if you think your item is bound to sell then you might want to choose a three- or a four-day auction. Conversely, if you think an item might have limited appeal and you have the patience, go for a longer auction. You can always take the option to close such an auction as soon as you have your first bidder to get the transaction over sooner.

In the USA, regular sellers report that bidding levels drop during summer. In response, many lower their prices during these months, or move to a free listings site such as Yahoo to cut their losses.

Reserve auctions

Hated by bidders, but popular among sellers, a reserve price auction is where your minimum or reserve bid price is kept secret from the buyer. To kick things off, the bidding starts at a price lower than the minimum, in some cases as low as £1 or $1. If this minimum reserve price is not reached then, although the goods may have multiple bids, the seller is not obliged to go through with a deal.

There are two reasons, a cynical one and an honest one, for a seller placing such a reserve price. Firstly, a seller who wants to start a bidding war will place a stupidly low price to attract attention. Usually a few people are pulled in by this and place bids at the low price. After each bid is placed, the auction page should say whether the reserve has been met. In theory the seller hopes that by generating enough interest the reserve price will finally be met (and exceeded). A more honourable reason for a reserve price auction is where the seller is clueless as to the real market value of an item and wants to find out how much it reaches. Here the seller sets a suitably high reserve price and watches the bids the item attracts. If at the end of the auction the reserve is not met, the highest bid may still be of interest to the seller, who can then get in touch with that bidder to work out a deal.

Needless to say, many bidders dislike being toyed with in reserve price auctions and avoid them. However, if the item is of particular interest to the buyer then it might be worth emailing the seller and asking just what the reserve price is.

Promoting your auction

If your auction is really something special and you want as many people to know about is as possible, consider spending a little extra on promoting it. Most auction sites charge a small fee to have an item placed in one of their featured auction categories that appear at the top of each listing.

A cheaper approach might be to leave a message about your auction on an auction forum page or web ring related to the category you are selling in. Finally, in extreme cases, you might consider telling a newspaper about your auction. There has been a whole string of weird online auction stories over the last year and if your auction is weird enough then it just might work.

Trash for cash

For serious auctioneers nothing is too frivolous to be sold. In the USA someone once sold the dregs they found stuck below the cushions on their sofa for $7 through eBay. If it is priced attractively enough and presented well, almost anything can sell.

Do you have something 'valuable' to throw away that you no longer want? Old newspapers with famous headlines, ticket stubs to famous football matches or rock concerts, broken appliances that could be used for spare parts – all could sell. In the USA it is popular for adults to re-buy toys similar to the ones they owned in their youth. Others are attracted to collecting the original packaging for drinks and food from the same era. Old Coke bottles or Coca-Cola cans (notably ones with classic motifs, i.e. not spoilt by having adverts plastered all over them) are especially popular.

Selling to the USA US buyers often love the corniest things about the UK, such as royal memorabilia or toby jugs. Many UK traders do well out of selling British newspapers or magazines with articles and photos of pop or Hollywood stars unavailable in the USA. If your item is aimed at the USA, state a shipping price for sending your item there. Suggest special payment terms for US buyers and consider pricing the item in dollars too.

//DURING THE AUCTION

Depending on which site you use, your auction advert could either appear automatically on the site or, in the case of larger sites with more information to process, anything up to three hours later.

One of the most exciting parts of having your own auction is checking to see if you have any bids. To save time logging on to the site and then searching for your page, you can make a direct link on your desktop by right clicking on your mouse and choosing the 'Create a link' option. If your instincts go against cluttering your desktop, remember that these links can be easily removed to your recycle bin at the end of the auction.

eBay has the most advanced auction-checking software and offers other timesaving devices. If you are running several auctions, rather than creating a link for each, you have the option of going direct to their 'My eBay' link, which will list all your auctions on one page and tell you the number of bids on each and the amount reached.

Changing your descriptions

If you have left out vital information from your auction description, do not despair – you should be allowed to go back and add this mid-auction. Generally speaking, though, you will not be allowed to change the text you have already written; you may only add text. However, eBay allows wholesale changes to a description if it has received no bids. A warning though: if you add to an auction description, a bidder can use this as an excuse to withdraw their bid. If you cannot change your description, you have the option of cancelling the auction.

Closing an auction early

Cancelling an auction with no bids should be straightforward at most sites. All it is going to cost you is your listing fee. Cancelling an auction with bids on it, though, is unadvisable – you will open yourself up to receiving negative feedback from the person(s) who placed the bid(s). Even if you did not receive negative feedback, auction sites look down on such activity.

In some instances you may want to end an auction early, especially if you are happy with the top bid you have received. Many a time in an auction you will get a bid from someone with a high feedback rating, but who then loses out to someone with a low feedback rating at the auction's close. Closing an auction early can prevent this from happening, though be aware that, generally, you get most of your bids in the last few hours of an auction and therefore you might be doing yourself out of a better deal.

Bidders questions

It is a sensible strategy for bidders to ask questions before they place their bid. Some of these questions will surprise you and some may irritate you, but they all should be dealt with as quickly and politely as possible. The last thing you want is to be answering questions after the auction has ended.

Many bidders' questions will be casually phrased and without salutations; this is the prerogative of the bidder. Be warned though: casually phrased questions are often the sign of an inexperienced bidder or someone who may be problematic; do not be over-casual back because this will encourage a lax attitude.

Often bidders' questions will be the result of your not having provided a full description. Unclear or missing shipping and payment prices are a common cause of bidders' questions. Often too you will get searching questions about the quality of your item: Is it in good condition? Is it marked in any way? Does it have the original box? If you are selling an electronic device, many people will want to know about all the little extra buttons and sockets on it.

Keep an upbeat tone to your answers but, at the same time, do not try to bluff the bidders; if they have taken the initiative to ask the question in the first place, they are not stupid. Finally, answer questions quickly because if a seller does not answer a question there might be grounds for someone who has placed a bid to retract it.

Auction outages

The computers at auction sites go down occasionally and eBay often takes several-hour breaks for computer maintenance. If this happens in the last crucial minutes of an auction, it could lose you bids. This is annoying but, unfortunately, you have no grounds to complain. In the terms and conditions you signed when you registered, there is a clause exempting the auction site from blame for any such 'outages'. eBay, which has become notorious for its regular outages, will sometimes extend an auction by an extra day after an unusually lengthy outage.

Be patient Checking your auction every day only to see that it has got no bids can be disheartening. Do not get too worried though; statistics show that most bids take place on the last day of the auction. The last few hours of an auction are often the most exciting for a seller. You will find that sometimes, even when you have received no bids for almost seven days, your auction will suddenly become the site of a bidding war.

//AFTER THE AUCTION HAS ENDED

Be prepared. When the auction ends, the party is over for the seller and the hard work begins. Your first job is to maintain the excitement of the auction by sending an email out to the winning bidder ASAP. The buyer usually wants the deal to close as fast as you do, so a quick reply will set things off well. You will receive an official confirmation email from the auction site, but these often arrive several hours later. Do not wait for this if you have the opportunity. Email the winning bidder as soon as possible.

Write a positive email, congratulating the bidder on 'winning' the auction (it's corny but it works). Then give them all the information they need to send you your money. This includes the sale price of the auction plus shipping costs and your payment address. Ideally the buyer should contact you within three days, confirming these details. If at this stage you and the buyer need to iron out any payment or shipping technicalities, offer the buyer your telephone number – this will speed things along much faster than waiting to receive emails everyday. Once you have received payment, it is good etiquette to inform the buyer straight away and at the same time inform them of when you expect your package to reach them.

Finally, if you have given someone a good deal then it is natural to expect positive feedback in return. Often people will just forget to do this. Your best bet is to prompt people into leaving feedback by ending your last email message to a buyer with something along the lines of 'All successful transactions end in positive feedback'.

Building up contacts Not everyone enjoys the auction process. You may want to include in your email a message to the buyer offering them the chance to contact you directly for anything related that you have to sell.

Trade in categories like collectibles often provides great opportunities for making friends or good contacts; this can be one of the most rewarding aspects of online auctions.

Potential seller problems Dealing with professional auction users is usually a delight for the ease with which auctions can be completed. In the near future though, as regular auction users look set to double in the UK, you will often find yourself dealing with those who are new to auctions and so have not yet learned all the rules.

Many newcomers to auctions start out with irrational fears that the first person they deal with is going to scam them. It will be your job to allay such fears and this may take several emails to achieve. Of course, such newcomers represent a risk too. Their zero ratings could disguise someone who has assumed a new identity after receiving negative feedback on an old ID. You might want to take greater precautions with such buyers. If an item is valuable or rare, consider sending it by registered post. Not only is this a better guarantee of delivery, but it also insures against anyone attempting to scam you by saying that the item did not arrive. By the way, it is the seller's responsibility to claim insurance if the item does not arrive.

Relisting As around half of all the items do not sell, if more than half of your auctions are unsuccessful then you are clearly doing something wrong. There are no big rules here; basically, when you come to relist the item, consider changing anything or everything. The winning factor you need could be a new description, a lower price, a better photo, a new title, a different category, another auction site, cheaper shipping terms or even ending the auction on a different day of the week.

Returns Although sellers dread them, returns will happen occasionally. Your initial reaction might be to deny everything and hold on to the money, but this will open you up to negative feedback.

If you have not been clear and honest with your description, a buyer has a legitimate right to ask for their money back. However, the buyer too has an obligation to act in a businesslike fashion. They should email you first before sending anything back and they should also do this within three days of receiving the goods. If you care about your feedback ratings and consider that maybe the buyer is right, wait for the item to come back and then refund the money.

Occasionally when a buyer has a complaint, the seller is not at fault. The buyer may have misread your description and ended up with something different to what they expected. Many who buy second-hand goods do so under the misapprehension that what they are buying is in mint condition. Do not encourage this idea.

The anatomy of a deadbeat bidder

The biggest danger for a buyer is getting robbed, while the biggest for a seller is a buyer who does not complete the deal. Such buyers are known as deadbeats. This may simply be a buyer who does not reply to your emails, a buyer who does not send you any money or one who sends you a cheque that bounces.

There are numerous explanations for deadbeats: some are disorganised, some are malicious, some might have got caught up in a competitive bidding war and overbid, some might have changed their minds, some might be children who are bidding as a prank, some might have lost their memory, some might be compulsive shoppers who cannot afford to pay and some might have accidentally let their dog bid for them. Sometimes it is impossible to know why because they simply do not contact you. The worst deadbeats, though, are the ones that come up with broken promises and excuses. They might claim to be too busy, to have lost their job, to be able to pay you only at the end of the month.

The only acceptable way for a bidder to back out of a deal after an auction has ended is if they have emailed you with a polite, persuasive, believable and, most importantly, speedy explanation that they cannot complete the deal. In such cases you may feel that posting a neutral rather than a negative feedback is a fair response.

Dealing with deadbeats

An early warning sign of a deadbeat is someone with a spotty feedback rating. If you have such a bidder, be firm. It is commonly accepted that if a buyer does not contact you within three days of an auction's close, then the seller is at liberty to contact the second-highest bidder and offer to sell to them. The longer you wait for the deadbeat to contact you, the less chance you have of persuading the second-highest bidder to do a deal – for which they are under no obligation to complete.

If your deadbeat is your only bidder, you will have to be more patient. If after three days they have not contacted you, send them an email requesting that they contact you within your own specified time limit or else you will consider the auction cancelled and post negative feedback. Such a policy might suggest an unforgiving view of human nature and the first time you encounter such a bidder, you might be tempted to give them the benefit of the doubt. The second time it happens though, follow the above guidelines.

Legally a deadbeat buyer has broken a signed agreement and the seller can sue, but lawyers and solicitors are probably going to be the only beneficiaries of such actions. If at any time during a deal you feel that contacting the bidder directly would be more beneficial, you can request your auction site to give you the bidder's telephone number. An auction site should cancel fees for an auction that has fallen through. Lastly, if you wish to block any future bids from someone you know to be a deadbeat bidder, you should be able to arrange this with your auction site.

If you have any further queries about how to get the best from your auction sites, the following customer support services might be useful: at eBay **support@ebay.com** should, in theory, get back to you within 24 hours; the customer support address at QXL is **help@qxl.com**.

//PHOTOS

An auction lacking an image is not only less likely to sell – it is also less likely to go for a high price. Arguably items such as CDs, computer software and books can sell perfectly well without images, as their looks are not paramount; however, as a general rule, an item with an image indicates that it is being sold by someone who is a committed seller.

To a buyer hesitant about fraud, an image is tangible proof that your item exists. Furthermore, an attractive image will trigger acquisitive impulses in buyers' brains and encourage them to bid higher.

Creating the image

The first step is to get your image on to your computer. Consider trying any of the following methods, remembering always to save the image as either a JPEG or a GIF file and to save it to your desktop.

Disk You may not have realised it, but any decent photo-developing shop will be able to process an ordinary camera film and put it on to a disk (a typical price is around £11 ($16.50) for processing up to 25 photos). Once you have the disk you should be able to upload the photos and save them to your desktop.

Digital camera If you have got one of these then you are laughing. These can be connected direct to your computer to download photos. The cost of the cheapest digital camera at **www.jungle. com** is around £200 ($300), though you might well pick up a cheaper one at a merchant auction where they are popular items. Second-hand prices for digital cameras from eBay are regularly around the £50 ($75) mark.

Video A modern video camera should connect to a computer in the same way as a digital camera.

Scanner A scanner is perfect for flat paper items, books, CDs, watches, cards and videos but when used to copy a photo it will lose some image quality.

Taking the photo Try to give your photo an uncluttered backdrop. A plain wall, carpet or a sheet will provide this. For any unusual items where scale cannot be easily guessed at, place an everyday item such as a coin next to it.

Editing the image A scanner comes with software that allows you to manipulate your images. Alternatively, your computer might have image-editing software already installed. It is recommended that you save your image at a size of 50KB or less; any more and you will be stuck with an image that takes ages to download.

Uploading images At the time of writing, eBay is the only top site that does not allow the uploading of images direct to its pages.

They are at present planning to change this and by the time you read this, all may well have changed. Fortunately, QXL, Yahoo and Amazon have made uploading images an easy process. On their 'create an auction' pages, the press of a button uploads the icons on your desktop, from where you can select the photos you have already saved there.

Image-hosting sites

For sites that do not allow you to upload images directly, you will need to host your images at special service sites on the net. Be warned: do not attempt such a process speedily or you will end up beating your fists against your keyboard in frustration. This is never an easy process and many sites make a real hash of explaining it (the simplest method is to be found at **www.auctionwatch.com**).

Assuming you have chosen to do this at Auctionwatch, your first step is to register. You will then have to wait for a confirmation email and password from them before you can use their site. When you come back to log on to Auctionwatch, click on the members' section and then go to 'Image Hosting'. Here Auctionwatch can browse your desktop (where you have saved your image) and download it to the site. However, the process of downloading can take time, especially if your image is large, so it is best done at off-peak times. Once the photo has downloaded you will be given a set of HTML with details of your photo. Cut and save this and then paste it on to the description page at your auction site. In return for this service you will be asked to display a little Auctionwatch logo on your auction screen.

A potential problem here is that if your image host's website crashes then your image will temporarily disappear too.

4//SECURITY

What is to stop someone just taking my money and not bothering to send anything in return? This is the main and justifiable fear of people taking part in any form of e-commerce.

At present, fraud is rare and fortunately most of us using online auction sites are just everyday people looking to buy or sell bargains. If anything, the feedback system at most sites encourages people to act in a more professional manner than in your average e-commerce transaction. If Amazon sends your book a week late, they are not going to let you post a message on their site telling them what idiots you think they are.

Though fraud does happen, it is commonly stated that if it were as rampant as some might suspect then, for example, eBay would not be logging the 400,000 new auctions it receives every day. eBay has officially stated that out of every of 25,000 purchases on their site only 0.003% of buyers are defrauded. Another source states that 'Less than one hundredth of a percent of the millions of transactions conducted on eBay have resulted in a fraud complaint and eBay takes every one seriously'. Some are sceptical of these figures and claim they are too low, but the point should be taken that, on the whole, fraud is rare.

When auction sites are there to help
The good news on auction fraud is that the top auction sites are increasingly competing with each other to offer better anti-fraud insurance. Amazon and eBay both offer insurance to the buyer who has been defrauded and lost their money.

eBay's Safe Harbour scheme insures bidders against non-receipt of their products up to a maximum of $200 in the USA and £120 in the

UK. However, this deal does not apply if you buy from someone with a negative rating or if you have a negative rating yourself. Also, the insurance does not cover you if the item has been lost in transit, in which case it is the seller's responsibility. This part of the eBay site can also provide you with 'real world' contact details of the person you have sent the money to and it is also the place where you report 'questionable activity'.

Amazon has an A–Z guarantee worth $250 or £150 for all those using its Amazon payments system. This is a bidder protection scheme for those 'whose item does not arrive or where it is materially different'.

When auction sites do not get involved

Beyond offering insurance for buyers, most auction sites will go to great lengths to remove themselves from getting involved in buyer–seller disputes. This is partly a practical response, as they could not afford to be personally answerable to every dispute. It is also a protection against being drawn into any expensive legal cases.

Many auction sites portray themselves as merely the owners of a trading hall, for which they charge a small fee for people to enter and do business. Such statements can be found in their terms and conditions, which often go to almost comical lengths to protect sites against being drawn into any disputes. The following segment is typical.

> You agree to release us from any claims, demands, losses and damages of any kind known and unknown, suspected and unsuspected, disclosed and undisclosed, that you may have arising out of or in any way connected with such disputes.

Not everyone is happy about such policies. A look at the forum pages of Auctionwatch will reveal a pile of furious complaints about eBay's lack of action against known or reported fraudsters operating on its site. A common complaint on these pages is that filing for mail fraud is more effective than complaining to eBay. A recent case in the USA involved a group of buyers who bought fake autographs through eBay. They took eBay to court and claimed that the company knew the autographs to be fakes. The legal battles are still being fought and so, for the time being, most of the responsibility for sorting out such disputes lies with you.

Online Mediators The misunderstandings, character conflicts, demands for return of monies or goods and so on that can (and sometimes do) occur after an auction's close can only serve to sour the trade. If you cannot resolve the dispute then the 'impartial' mediators at Squaretrade (http://squaretrade.com) will offer to help out. Their service at present is only for eBay transactions over $100 made within the past month. The mediation process takes place online, with both parties encouraged to submit their version of events before advice is given. Finally, an agreement contract is drawn up and presented to both parties. The site claims disputes are typically resolved within ten days. There is no mention of fees on the site.

Preventing fraud
If the auction companies will not protect you then you must look after yourself. The following are all sensible guidelines.

1 Do not enter into expensive deals with sellers whose feedback rating is low. Be extra careful when dealing with
   someone who has a history of regular negative feedback.

2   Anything that sounds too good to be true probably is. Trust your intuition. Best of all, check the seller's feedback records; the dodgiest-looking items are usually sold by sellers with low feedback ratings.

3   If a fraudster is caught, they risk losing their email account. For this reason they are less likely to register with an Internet provider such as CompuServe, Demon, BT or Claranet, where they have to pay a fee and register a credit card. Creating an assumed identity is much easier at free email sites such as Hotmail, Freeserve and Yahoo.

4   Buying from overseas is always riskier, not least because such fraud committed abroad is harder to pursue. At present there is no clear law on which country's judicial system applies in the cases of international Internet fraud.

5   If you are the victim of fraud and wish to report it, you will need copies of all the emails in your transaction. It is a good routine to regularly store such emails in a special auction deals mail folder.

Credit cards The main rule when using your credit card on the Net is not to send your details by email because these are at risk of being intercepted by a third party. The only places you should use your card number is on the payment pages at merchant auction sites or on an auction site's registration form. In each case make sure that the site has encrypting security features such as Secure Sockets Layer (SSL). When you view a page at such a secure server, a padlock or a key will be displayed at the bottom of the page. If the key is broken or the lock is open, so is the security. In a secure area, the web address should start **https://** rather than **http://**. The

SSL device scrambles your card number as it is sent, making it impossible for it to be intercepted.

Scam alert

Below is a list of some of the most common scams at online auctions. The bulletin boards at eBay are regularly posted with details of any new scams doing the rounds.

- You are about to win an auction and, before the real seller contacts you, you get an email from a scamster claiming to be the seller and asking you to forward money to them.

- Auctions that scream at you in BIG CAPITAL LETTERS!! are more likely to be scams than ordinary adverts.

- Two buyers work in tandem to buy your item at a low price. Firstly, bidder A places a low bid on an item then, secondly, bidder B places a bid so high that it scares off all other bidders for the duration of the auction. Finally, minutes before the auction's close, bidder B retracts their bid, making bidder A the rightful winner at a bargain price.

- An independent report suggested that fakes account for more than a third of the luxury goods on the Net. You are more likely to be scammed buying a Rolex than a Swatch.

If you suspect a scam, report it to the site, which should investigate and take action. If you want the advice of other auction users at eBay, there is a user-to-user Q & A forum (you can find this link under the Help heading on the site map), which might help you reach a decision over any potentially dodgy deal.

Dealing with merchant auctions

Generally speaking, buying from merchant auctions should be less risky than buying from individuals. The safest companies, though, are the ones you know best. If you are unfamiliar with the company, consider the following advice. The most secure auction sites are full of reassurances on every page about how safe they are. They will provide links to escrow services and offer guarantees. If you have doubts about the company, ask yourself if are you absolutely sure the company are who they say they are. The most reputable websites will include real world contact details such as an address and a telephone number. These details are sometimes hard to find but are usually listed in a site's terms and conditions. If you are suspicious, try the phone number to see if it is real.

Guaranteed sites

To counter fears of online fraud, many reputable online companies have let themselves be monitored by independent companies, whose certificates they then display at the foot of their home page.

The two biggest suppliers of certificates are Verisign and Thawte. Verisign is the leading provider of Internet trust services and ensures that all data transferred to a website is encrypted, thus protecting against disclosure to third parties. Thawte also verifies SSL connections and security for credit cards.

The Public Eye verification company goes one step further by allowing customers of the sites that bear their certificate to report back on what they think of that company. Companies end up with a 1–5 star ranking based on these customer feedbacks. These reports can be viewed by visiting www.publiceye.com.

In the UK, the Consumers' Association has introduced the Which? Web Trader Scheme to encourage consumer confidence on the

Net. Those who bear the Web Trade Scheme certificate agree to abide by its code of practice. This stipulates that the site is secure and that the Consumers' Association will compensate anyone who loses money through dealing with the site. The code of practice also ensures that all members agree to a policy of customer refunds, guarantees and dealing with complaints in a fair way.

//KNOWING YOUR RIGHTS

Buying from online stores in the UK does not mean you give up any of your statutory rights. Goods must fit their description and be of a satisfactory quality. If you find yourself in dispute with an online site, you can contact the following organisations.

Office of   **www.oft.gov.uk/**
Fair Trading   **html/shopping/index.html**

'If you have a valid complaint, you have the right to have the problem sorted out' is the reassuring tone taken by this site. If it feels like a David and Goliath battle getting your money back from merchant auctions that have ripped you off, this site will help put you at ease. Amazingly for a government document, this is all written in easy-to-understand English. The site provides links to Citizens' Advice Bureaus, Trading Standards officers and ombudsmen and explains each of their roles. The site also encourages the use of these services before taking a matter to court, although it does give details of how to take a company to court and the likely costs involved.

BBC Watchdog   **www.bbc.co.uk/watchdog**
This site has a store of bad customer experiences, some relating to online auctions. It also gives you the chance to log your complaint and have it featured in the television show of the same name.

Fraud.com **www.fraud.com**

This US site worryingly states that fraud at online auctions consti-
tutes the greatest number of fraud cases online. Here you can learn
about common Internet scams, one of which warns against fraud-
ulent sellers who have had positive feedback planted in their
ratings to encourage honest buyers to bid in their auctions. Here
you can also report any cases you have come across of online
fraud. Fraud.com is funded by the US National Consumers League,
a private non-profit-making group.

Scambusters **www.scambusters.org**

Short and direct, this site hates Internet fraud and provides direct
links to such pages as 'Tell Us Your Scam Experience' and 'Internet
Scam Archives'. Full of good, strong advice such as 'If it's a spam,
it's a scam' and why you should avoid businesses with anonymous
users. One interesting scam reported here is the auction of rare,
limited-edition Furbies. As it happens, the manufacturers of Furbies
ensure there have never been any limited editions of their toys.

The Better Business Bureau **www.bbb.com**

US online companies' records can be checked up on a state-by-
state basis here, though it looks a long-winded process. You can
also file complaints about US companies.

International Web Police **www.web-police.org**

'The largest crime fighting agency on the net' apparently, but a
rather dubious-looking site.

//HOW YOUR PRIVACY IS PROTECTED (OR NOT)

Spam Registering is free, as many auction sites like to tell us, yet
often it may not be as innocent as that. Frequently, by giving away
your email address, you can leave yourself open to spam, the web's

nickname for 'junk mail'. These tiresome little messages are usually offering to sell you stuff that you do not want or making crazy claims on how you can 'Make $3,000 a Day Without Working'.

Before you hand over personal information, make quite sure that the site you are registering with has a privacy policy in place (its normally in the 'Help' or 'Customer Policy' pages). Such a policy should state that your personal information will not be sold on or generally used to send you unsolicited mail. Some sites will give you the option over whether you would like to receive details of promotional offers or not. This option usually comes as a default, so to stop the mailings simply tick the box provided.

The top auction sites are well aware of the unpopularity of spam and so try to keep such messages to their members at a minimum. They also take a dim view of people who use the sites to send spam messages to their members. If you are bothered by such email, you should report it to the customer service address at the relevant site.

Cookies Cookies are small files created by a website to store information about your preferences for that site. These files are stored on your computer's hard disk and when you revisit a site they remember your preferences (e.g. searches and categories) and can customise your view of the site accordingly. They can also remember information you typed into the site, such as your email or home address.

5//GOING, GOING, GONE

//SHIPPING

The basics

Selling an item is a thrill, but packing and shipping it is a drag, especially if you have not given it any thought until the auction is over. Your most important piece of research on shipping is finding the exact price. If you have agreed a shipping price with a buyer and you get to the post office to discover that it costs more, you are going to lose out.

Remember to calculate your packaging costs too. Envelopes, brown tape, jiffy bags, boxes, polystyrene and bubble wrap might be needed. If you think packaging will be costly, discuss it with the buyer. On occasions you might be able to salvage some of this material from old packages. If an item is second-hand, people will not expect it to arrive in a pristine white box, although a scruffy box that is falling apart and badly packed will create a bad impression. Some buyers may also be insulted by the use of old shopping bags as insulation, but newspaper is generally acceptable.

When in doubt, try to package your parcel neatly and responsibly. This is around the time the buyer is going to post you feedback, so you need to make a good impression. It is also a good idea to enclose a note confirming your seller name and contact details; a brief note along the lines of 'I hope you enjoy this product' helps too. After sorting out prices and packaging, it is considered professional to let your buyer know how long it will take for the package to arrive

Other factors to consider here include insurance. If an item is valuable or irreplaceable, send it by registered post. If shipping such items abroad, consider using a professional company like FedEx, whose packages are automatically insured.

Advanced Tips Keeping some scales at home and a price list of postage rates will save on trips to the post office to find out this kind of information.

Shipping companies

The courier company market is a competitive one and each company will make strong claims for its services. However, no company is infallible, despite whatever it claims to the contrary. Also bear in mind that delivery times can be a big problem. You cannot expect a person to wait in the whole day to sign for a parcel. Consider the option of having the parcel sent to your buyer's workplace.

The following companies are popular among online auction users.

Royal Mail   **www.royalmail.com**
An essential and easy-to-use site. Choose from eighteen types of mail service, all simply explained, ranging from good old ordinary first and second class to Swiftair, special delivery and registered. Next, pick a destination and then use the onsite calculator to type in the weight of your package and find out how much your delivery will cost. Simple.

DHL Worldwide Express   **www.dhl.co.uk**
DHL offers one- to two-day express deliveries of parcels to the USA. A 500 gramme parcel from the UK costs £31 (about $46) to New York and £36.65 (about $55) elsewhere in the US. Along with the price comes free packaging and tracking.

UPS www.ups.com

UPS specialise in international delivery. Their site offers a time calculator telling you how long its parcels should take to arrive, a tracking service, free packaging and all the necessary contact details for its local UK branches. It does not show prices though.

Fedex www.fedex.com

If a package has to get to the USA fast, this site offers a next-day service at £54.50 (about $82) for packages weighing 500 grammes; a two-day service will cost £26.50 (about $40). All packaging is free with the service and can be sent out to you specially.

//CUSTOMS AND VAT

Buying from abroad could be so much fun if it were not for the burdens of import and export duties and VAT. The good news is that some goods and countries are exempt. Goods transferred within the EU and goods bought under the value of £18/$27 (£26/$39 for gifts) from non-EU countries do not incur duty. There is no duty or VAT on books and no duty on computers.

HM Customs and Excise (**www.hmce.gov.uk/bus/regions/dutyrate. htm**) provides information on import duties and VAT for goods coming into the UK although it does not explain why some goods are charged up to 17% duty rate while others are exempt. Goods that do not incur duty include cassette recorders, computers, faxes, skincare products, make-up, metal and wood furniture, pearl jewellery and radios. Meanwhile, antiques incur no duty but are charged 5% VAT. Where charged, duty rates vary: at the top end of the scale are such items as DVD players, CD players and TVs at 14%, bikes at 15% and shoes at 17%, while close to the bottom are CDs at 3.5%. Some of these duties are there to protect UK industries; some of them, though, are simply unfathomable. The really bad news is that all items that are charged duty are also charged extra VAT. If there is anything you are unsure about, you can call 020 8910 3744 to find out.

Avoiding paying duties is very tempting, but be warned: HM Customs and Excise have a policy of opening parcels with ambiguous or incomplete customs forms. Also be aware that it is the seller who incurs the penalties if customs forms are completed dishonestly (for instance, if an item is marked as a gift, it can be exempt from customs) and many US auction users resent being asked to lie on customs forms for this very reason.

Forum pages

These chat rooms for auction users can be a great source of tips, solidarity and gossip. They help build up a sense of community and for this reason every top online auction site on the Net encourages them. Sadly, however, most forums, or 'cafés' as they are sometimes called, are merely parade grounds for show-offs, braggarts and bores who spout the sort of general juvenilia you would not expect from those over the age of eighteen. In such an environment, genuine users with real concerns do not bother joining in.

Forums at online auction sites also suffer from the self-imposed censorship of members who do no want a ticking-off from the site for saying unfavourable things about it. The best auction forum pages out of a bad lot are found at **www.auctionwatch.com** and **www.popula.com**.

//AUCTION HELP

Online auctions have become so popular in the USA that a whole online support industry has grown up around them. These range from sites offering valuations, auction software or auction news to independent auction forums where people can mouth off with impunity about how their favourite auction site has let them down again. Some of the help sites are listed below.

The best

Auctionwatch   www.auctionwatch.com

Simply one of the web's great sites. Probably its best feature is the forum pages, which allow free comment for users of top auction sites such as eBay, Amazon, Yahoo and more. Here buyers and sellers get to mouth off about their bad experiences with these sites. A common topic is the knocking of eBay, which often gets referred to as eGreed. You will also find a guide to using online auctions, news, item searches, image hosting, free counters and an antique and collectibles price appraisal service at $19.95 (about £13) per item.

Auction Works   www.auctionworks.com

If you are planning on a lot of Internet auctions then this site will be one of your best friends. It provides you with free image hosting, free counters, buyer and seller advice, shipping tips and can help you create your own temporary auction site with its own URL. It also has the best online auction news page.

Eppraisals   www.eppraisals.com

A wonderfully helpful and straightforward site that is, in its own words, 'a fast, easy and affordable service for learning more about what you have and what it is worth'. A team of online experts are given a digital photo of your prized antique and will email you back an 'eppraisal document' stating its US dollar value in return for a $20 (£13) fee. As the site points out, this 'document' can also be used as a proof of the item's worth and also for use in insurance claims. Examples of such assessments can be viewed on the site.

The site guides you through the description process and offers a step-by-step guide on how to send the image online.

The rest

Auction Designer   www.auctiondesigner.com

Use the software here to give your adverts their own unique look, with easy-draw colours and designs. For those who regularly auction in the same category, this could help you raise your profile, or at the very least make your ads look prettier than everyone else's. The software comes as a CD-ROM at $59.95 (£40) and comes with six months' free image hosting and counters.

Auctionguide   www.auctionguide.com

This offshoot of the *Chicago Tribune* keeps you up to date with the business news on the online auction sector, mainly who is buying whom and who is suing whom.

Auction Rover   www.auctionrover.com

Auction Rover lets you perform searches across an impressive-sounding 800 auctions, though many of these are pretty duff. Also some rather lame forum pages, news and advice.

Auction Tribune   www.auctiontribune.com

Online auction news of who is suing whom, who is acquiring and merging and who has got new business ideas. Also a long directory of auction sites and separate links pages for auction help sites.

The Collecting Channel   www.collectingchannel.com

A US online magazine and resource centre for antiques and collectibles. Here you will find pages on antiques, glass and pottery, stamps and coins, collectibles, jewellery and gems, toys and dolls, entertainment and sports. Each page contains short, snappy articles and links to current auctions of interest. The site also has its own chat rooms, message boards, wanted ads, grading service and quizzes.

Esmarts.com   **www.esmarts.com/auctions**
Often pointless but fun top-five rankings of all kinds of sites, including online auctions. The rankings on which auction sites are judged are best, hot, super (!), best for business-to-business, best for computers and best non-general site. There is an auction forum link here too.

Honesty   **www.honesty.com**
Not everyone who views your auction places a bid on it. If you want to know how much interest your auction is generating, Honesty's free counters will do the job. A further service will also tell you at what times they are browsing. Also image hosting.

Image Host   **www.imagehost.com**
Professional-looking site that will host your first image free, but thereafter charges a fee.

Internet World News   **www.internetworldnews.com**
Financial Times news on Internet businesses. For those interested in acquisitions and mergers only.

The Online Auction Users Organisation   **www.auctionusers.org**
This site's aim is to create a pressure group for honest and reputable auction users. It campaigns against illegal or bad auction practices, warns of fraud and plans to create a 'good auction user' certificate for honourable users. This is a worthy enterprise that at present lacks character; particularly its forum pages lack any real discussion.

Page To Go   **www.pagetogo.com**
If the help sites here are not enough, this site provides a large directory of similar sites.

Picture Bay Pbay   **www.pbay.com**

At the time of writing, this company was negotiating with eBay to
become the authorised image host providers for its auctions. Pbay
boasts that it will upload photos from your desktop and then re-
format and resize them so that they are optimised for auction
viewing.

PixHost   **www.pixhost.com**

Images hosted at 50 cents (about 33p) for 30 days. This, thankfully,
is a simple guide to uploading images to auctions, with a great
tutorial page on how to edit your images. New users are given two
free photos on signing up. It says 'We strongly recommend that
you keep your images under 32KB so that your potential buyers see
your image quickly' and it will actually refuse to process images
over 50KB.

Richard   **www.samizdat.com/ebay.html**
Seltzer   **www.samizdat.com/ebay2.html**

Here, Richard Seltzer, a long-term eBay trader, Internet journalist
and author, has written two guides aimed at those selling
collectibles. His experience suggests that people are very trustworthy when dealing with low-cost items (anything under $20/ £13)
and he recommends that a seller should send such items before
receiving payment. This practice, he says, will ensure a better
rapport and positive feedback. He is also a great believer in ending
auctions at weekends.

Shecollects.com   **www.shecollects.com**

A light-hearted site full of tips for those buying and selling
collectibles. One of its best features is its enormous links page.

Worthguide   **www.worthguide.com**

A must for online auction addicts; here you can find what can only be described as league tables on the popularity of items in online auctions everywhere. On our viewing there was the thrilling news that Maple the Canadian teddy bear was the most popular Beanie Baby sold that week, accounting for $1,740.36 (about £1,149) worth of trade. For the market as a whole, Worthguide reveals that Beanies and Pokémon-related items shift the greatest number of units, while the biggest value in terms of money was for all things electronic.

Payment services

Bid Pay   www.bidpay.com

A well-established US site that allows you to generate a money order online, which is then sent directly to your seller, saving time and money. A simple and attractive service, the site informs it is planning to go international 'in the near future'.

PayPal   www.paypal.com

This vastly popular US payment site is planning to offer its service internationally some time in 2000. Proof that the best ideas are the most simple, all PayPal does is act as a credit card go-between for buyers and sellers. This eliminates the lengthy wait for cheques to clear and the risky business of sharing your credit card details with strangers. All this and there is no charge. PayPal makes its money by working like a bank and investing the money it has slushing around between deals. PayPal accepts both Visa and MasterCard.

Price comparison sites

Bottom Dollar   www.bottomdollar.com

A US site that finds out the cheapest prices available online for new consumer goods. The service is linked to both US and UK shopping sites. Going by the good write-ups the site has had from computer magazines, this is the place to come for computer bargains. The drawback to this service is that you cannot search by enough subcategories, which makes search results overlong.

Check A Price   www.checkaprice.com

'The ultimate UK comparison site', as it bills itself, is one of the easiest to use. Its strengths are in its price comparisons for computers and consumer electronics.

Price Checker   www.pricechecker.co.uk

Checks UK prices under the categories of music, books, games, computers, films and utilities (gas and electricity).

Price Scan   www.pricescan.com

Large and effective US site that describes itself as an 'unbiased guide to the lowest prices'. Its strength lies in its precise search abilities. For example, a portable TV can be chosen by category and from here you can state a maximum price and have the option of specifying a manufacturer, size and functions too. The search result for the cheapest portable by any manufacturer turns out to be a Memorex MTO500 with a 5-inch screen at $37.95 (£25) from www.1cache.com.

Shop Smart   www.shopsmart.com

UK service that checks prices under the categories of health and beauty, tickets and events, toys and games, clothes and fashion, and travel. The site also features some 3,000 reviews of online stores.

//AUCTION HELP SOFTWARE

In the USA it is estimated that 20% of those who sell on eBay gain the majority of their income from it. Many of these professionals run up to 100 auctions a week and find the process of tracking their auctions and placing adverts repetitive and time consuming. To ease this workload the following sites offer software that automatically tracks auctions and places adverts.

The best

Blackthorne Software
www.blackthornesw.com

Impressive site that claims that one out of every twenty auctions listed on eBay uses its services. Its top auction package at $59.95 (£40) provides a database for maintaining and tracking all your auctions. It will also write beautifully formatted listings, enhance your images, automatically fill in eBay forms, tell you the state of play for your live auctions and automatically send out emails and feedback. It does everything in fact, except search and destroy deadbeat bidders. This all comes on a CD-ROM and Blackthorne's boast is that it will not only save you loads of time, but also increase your sales. A cheaper service, the Auction ticker at $19.95 (£13), simply tracks your auctions, telling you the number of bids, the highest bid, and the name of highest bidder.

The rest

Auction Browser
www.auction-browser.com

Software for buyers; the auction browser will track auctions that you bid on, watch prices and warn you when an auction you are interested in is about to close.

Auction Poster
www.auctionposter.com

An auction poster is not something to hang on the wall; it is, in fact, what this site immodestly describes as the 'World's Most Powerful Online Selling Tool'. It offers your advert a wide range of design themes and layouts; it will automate repetitive tasks, host images and track and post auctions across a wide variety of sites, including the UK and US versions of eBay, Amazon and Yahoo. The service costs $2.50 (£1.67) a month or $29.95 (£20) a year.

Auction Tamer   www.auctiontamer.com

Aimed at buyers, the Auction Tamer sold by Envision Software at $19.95 (£13) will track auctions over numerous sites, saving you the trouble of having to browse each individually. It can link to top US auctions such as eBay, Yahoo, Excite and Amazon as well as the UK versions of the same sites.

Sam Cool   www.samcool.com

Sam Cool's top software package for sellers ($50/£33) will help you write flash and colourful adverts as well as automatically leaving feedback and posting adverts. The cheaper Advert Wizard ($14.95/£10) allows you to create attractive adverts in minutes and it also hosts images.

Setting up your own auction site?

Have you spotted an unfilled niche in the auctions market?

If you are not ready yet to splash out on custom-made software, consider the options taken by such small traders as Madelena Antiques and Meteorites.com. Both run successful and busy auctions through a link to eBay on their own website. The link takes them to a special bespoke eBay page that lists their auctions. This carries the attractions of not having to heavily promote your own site and having access to eBay's 15.8 million registered users.

The following sites offer auction design services, including off-the-shelf ready-made designs. To see more, do a search under auction software at Yahoo.com.

Auction Share   www.auctionshare.com

Software and services for those looking to build online auction sites.

Every Soft www.everysoft.com

The EveryAuction software available here lets you run a nice-looking, full-featured auction hosted from your own web page.

Instil www.auctionsoftware.co.uk

Instil describes itself as the leading provider of business-to-business live auction software and its persuasive, well-written site provides an online demonstration of its services.

Siebel www.opensite.com

American software design company with experience of setting up auctions for UK companies including Buystuff and Bidbusiness. All sites come with advanced bidding pages and good feedback rating systems.

Sunset Creations www.sunsetcreations.com

A Canadian company experienced at building auction websites.

//ESCROW

Escrow is a service that ensures buyers get the goods they have paid for, in return for a fee of around 4% of the transaction.

A step-by-step guide to an escrow deal

1   The escrow company acts as a neutral third party. First, it takes contact and auction details from both the buyer and seller.

2   The buyer authorises the escrow company to debit their credit card.

3   Upon receipt of the money, the escrow company instructs the seller to send the goods. At this stage, many escrow companies insist that the seller uses a secure shipping method that requires the buyer to sign for the goods.

4 The buyer notifies the escrow company upon receipt of the goods. The buyer has three days in which to do this. This three-day 'window' is important – it allows the buyer to make sure they are happy with what they have received.

5 The escrow company sends the money on to the seller either after the three days have elapsed or when the buyer makes contact, whichever comes first.

The benefits of escrow

An escrow deal wipes out any of the risks normally associated with online auctions. It allows for a secure and fast payment method and effectively provides the buyer with a guarantee that if they do not like the goods, they can send them back. There is a strong disincentive for the buyer to do this though, as they will not only have to pay for the return shipping, but they will also still incur the fee to the escrow company.

The escrow fee is usually worked out as a small percentage of the total cost of the item plus shipping. Although both the buyer and seller benefit from such deals, it is customary for the buyer to pay all the escrow charges. This is partly because it is easier for the escrow company to take money from the buyer, whose credit card details it already holds. It is also fair if you consider that the seller will have to pay a fee of a similar size to the company who hosted the auction.

Unlike online auction sites, many escrow companies will become involved in buyer-seller mediation.

Companies offering escrow services

At the time of writing, both QXL and Amazon offer their own attractive escrow services and eBay is planning to start such a service in the near future. With the exception of Itrustyou.com, the following companies are all based in the USA and are only of use to those trading with the USA.

Escrow.com   www.escrow.com

Useful for C2C transactions with the US sellers, this site charges a 3.85% fee for credit card transactions and 1.1% for cheques or money transfers. The buyer is allowed a five-day inspection period. A useful extra on the site is an automatic fee calculator.

Iescrow.com   www.iescrow.com

Iescrow 'welcomes transactions from outside the USA' and such ambition explains why it has become the largest provider of online escrow services, with over 100,000 registered users and deals with both Amazon and eBay. For UK users this site is only for buyers doing business with US sellers since it only pays out in US dollar cheques. Transactions up to $100 (£66) are charged a $2.50 (£1.65) fee, while those between $100 and $25,000 are charged 4% on all credit card transactions. The inspection period for this site has to be agreed between the buyer and seller.

Itrustyou.com   www.itrustyou.com

This UK escrow service (which began trading in 1999) charges the buyer 3.5% for a credit card transaction and 2% for a cheque transaction. For such deals the buyer gets a two-day acceptance period. This clear and easy-to-use site can be used for several European languages and currencies and also handles US dollar transactions.

Safebuyer
www.safebuyer.com

The higher the value of your deal with Safebuyer, the cheaper will be your fees. Up to $100 (£66) there is a $5 (£3.30) charge, whereas between $1,001 (£661) and $2,500 (£1,650) there is a $40 (£26.50) charge, which works out at between 1.5 and 2% for deals valued at $2,000-2,500 (£1,320-1,650). The acceptance period for such deals, though, is only 24 hours.

Tradesafe.com
www.tradesafe.com

This large US escrow site specialises in business-to-consumer deals and so it is useful for those buying from US merchant sites. It only accepts international deals over $1,200 (£800) for which the buyer pays a 3.5% fee. A drawback for UK users of the site is that its money-back guarantee (if the goods are 'materially different than what was promised') only applies to US citizens.

6//REGIONAL DIRECTORY

//UK

The UK online auction is going through a vast land-grab phase, where many companies, big and small, are trying their luck at establishing themselves. In order to build up a loyal customer base many are offering free or reduced listings and commission fees for limited periods, but this cannot last for long (eBay started charging in July 2000) and only Yahoo looks like holding with its policy of free listings.

At present there are too many UK general auction sites offering the same kind of service and not all will survive. If the UK market follows that of the USA then over the next year or two a few companies will pull away from the pack (with eBay looking the only clear winner at present), building up their listings while the smaller companies dwindle and fail.

The best

---

eBay UK   www.ebay.co.uk

eBay UK may have arrived two years after QXL, but on its launch in October 1999 it had the immediate advantage of the most advanced online auction software package on the Net. Even without the massive publicity of QXL, in the space of about six months it established itself as the number one British site by a mile. It has achieved this status and reputation (like its US operation) largely through word of mouth. At present it has the largest consumer-to-consumer listings in the UK, at around 107,000 in total.

The attraction is obvious; eBay's pages are simple and attractive. To see your auctions listed on this big colourful site is a thrill in the way it never is at QXL. You are also offered more search functions and more general on-site help than anywhere else. Its feedback system too is the most popular and advanced on the net and has the added attraction of making dealing on its US site easier. Unlike QXL, eBay's purpose is clear, that is, to concentrate on consumer-to-consumer auctions alone.

As with its US operation, eBay's strength in the UK lies mainly with collectibles and the arts. A look at recent listings showed its largest categories as: books, film and music (44,000 auctions); general collectibles (20,807 auctions); toys (12,000 auctions); sports (10,000 auctions); computers and games (6,010 auctions); and coins and stamps (5,000 auctions).

Safe Harbour

eBays Safe Harbour scheme, pioneered in 1999, looks to be setting an example that will be followed by all other auction sites. Its main attraction is the insurance it offers to bidders who pay for something that is never sent, or for buyers who receive an item 'that is less than what is described'. This covers all deals up to the value of £120 ($180). Needless to say, the process of getting this money does not look easy and lengthy checks have to take place before this happens. Safe Harbour is also set up like an on-site detective agency in order to investigate customer reports about members who might be involved in fraudulent activity, feedback extortion, offers to sell feedback, bid manipulation, unwelcome bids, false identities and abusive language.

---

eBay's one major drawback has been its regular system outages – periods of up to several hours when the site is not available. These are the Internet equivalent of track maintenance on the railway. Partly they are caused by the fast expansion of eBay and the struggle of its computers to catch up. They are also there to allow better systems to be installed. Such is the importance of eBay in the US that the largest outages have made the national news. Recently these outages have taken place on the UK site between 9 a.m. and 1 p.m. on Fridays. Updates on the exact timing of these are posted at the bottom of the home page. The official line from eBay is that these outage will become smaller and smaller to the point that they may eventually just take place for a few minutes at 9 a.m. on Friday mornings. We shall see.

The best second-hand record store in the world

eBay's enormous range of CDs, records and tapes offer the best chance you will ever find of tracking down those deleted and rare releases. Adding the UK and USA listings together, you have access to around 150,000 CDs and 130,000 vinyl records. The added advantage these listings have over a high-street second-hand record store is that there is near complete turnover of stock every week. A search on even the most obscure and unloved of bands often brings surprising results (e.g. four entries for early 80s indie band the Au Pairs).

The awesome size of the eBay site is not immediately apparent from its home page, which simply features its most popular applications. To get a good idea of what it can do for you, have a look at its site map. This page is often a source of surprising features that you never knew existed. For example, on the US site there are the bargain-basement and big-ticket categories; the former has a gallery of some of the cheapest or best-value items on the site and the latter has the most expensive items, including houses and expensive cars.

The final pièce de résistance of the eBay experience is that, even if you cannot find what you are looking for, you do not have to keep checking every week; eBay's personal shopper page lets you leave details of up to three items, which will be recognised by the site as soon as an auction for any of them is listed at the site. When this happens, you will be informed by email.

Firedup www.firedup.com

The UK's top merchant and promotional auction site was born with a silver spoon in its mouth. Owned by News International, it enjoys regular plugs in the *Sun*, *The Times* and the *Sunday Times* newspapers. Consequently, Firedup is a source of weekly headline-grabbing auctions such as a date with one of the Sun's page 3 girls, Posh Spice's wedding crown (solid gold with 231 diamonds) and a yacht from the James Bond movie *The World is not Enough*.

Beyond such razzmatazz, most auctions on the site come from ordinary high-street retail operations, with categories ranging from books to clothes, computers, cars, property and travel. Many items, probably end-of-line or surplus stock, start from £1, such as Ralph Lauren sweaters. There are also lots of UK travel breaks in hotels at Brighton, Blackpool, Scarborough and Margate. There are PCs with 32MB SD RAM from £495 ($743) and high-profile items included a Vauxhall Corsa, last seen at £4,100 ($6150) with 54 bids. For the *Sunday Times* readers there is also some posh stuff such as some surprisingly good modern art paintings, signed books by big-name authors and classic photos from the *Sunday Times* photo library, such as a fantastic shot of the top of Mount Everest from a biplane in 1933 at £175 ($262). One attractive feature is that, when registering, you do not have to give credit card details; this is solely between you and the individual merchant listed at the site.

fsauctions www.fsauctions.co.uk

Freeserve auctions has gained all its attention from its innovative merchant auction offers, such as cars from Europe at UK price-busting levels. Other notable auctions on its site include Thistle Hotels offering numerous UK breaks and a company called the £10 Shop, all of whose auctions start at £10 including three shirts, a Kookai bag, a kettle and 5 CDs. Looking at the home page you may not have guessed that it had any C2C auctions at all, but they can be found, though, on some surprisingly badly designed pages.

QXL www.qxl.co.uk

QXL has ridden its luck for sometime, benefiting from a slew of largely positive publicity that has placed it in the public's collective consciousness as the number one UK site.

It lacks much, though, when compared to eBay. Its most apparent fault is its design. The dominant grey graphics, along with the slow links, awkward site navigation, lack of subcategories and tiny print, take all the fun out of browsing this site. Also, because of the lack of category breakdown, it is advisable to use the search function at all times. Such problems are fixable, but the site also suffers from an identity crisis; it cannot decide whether it is going to be a merchant auction site with amazing offers and bargains from famous brands and retailers, or whether it is going to be a site catering to the British public's desire for an online auction site, where they can auction off their unwanted junk. It ends up doing neither very well.

The best value at present on QXL lies in its merchant auctions. These take pride of place on the home page, effectively putting the consumer-to-consumer auction on a lower status. There have been one-off deals with British Midland, a proposed deal with Blockbuster videos to sell ex-rental videos, a contract to sell off Wembley stadium bit by bit and a current deal with Majestic Wine to auction boxes of wine. All deals come with a fourteen-day money-back guarantee. Its consumer listings are often of dubious quality since many of its figures are bolstered by listings from its other European sites. Therefore, although recently across its entire European operations it held 204,118 auctions, for the UK user many of these auctions would involve the unpalatable prospect of doing business across a wide range of European currencies and languages. However, it is helpful that QXL puts UK listings first on every category page. At present the largest listings by category are for CDs and Beanies, with 24,000 and 6,000 auctions respectively.

Unlike eBay, QXL has made expansion into Europe its number one priority, though for the typically Eurosceptic British this does not appear to offer as much value as does access to US listings at eBay, Yahoo and Amazon.

One step in the right direction for QXL is its 'Safe Pay/SafeShip' offer that is an all-in-one escrow and door-to-door courier service. It places the charge on the successful bidder, who pays 5% of a winning bid, or at least £4 ($6). In return, the buyer gets a four-day approval period. All payments are through debit or credit cards. If they can get this right then why not the rest of the site?

Yahoo Auctions   http://uk.auctions.yahoo.com
Yahoo's policy of a lo-fi, low-maintenance site offering little customer support in return for free auctions is a happy trade-off for many and means that you always get a large number of listings. Free ads encourage people not only to make multiple listings using

the site's 'bulk loader' function but also to try their luck with items perhaps unlikely to sell. However, the trade-off for sellers is that Yahoo Auctions' lack of quality in listings leads to a much lower bid rate than eBay. At present the 54,000 listings on the UK site are bolstered by US sellers who have clicked the 'International bidders welcome' box.

One outcome of the low-maintenance policy and free ads is that Yahoo Auctions is the source of a great many pornographic and other semi-legal-looking auctions. Pranksters also love the site, setting up spoof auctions for their own amusement, but do not worry – these are easy to spot.

Good features on the site include some helpful category break-downs; for example, from 7,000 antiques and collectibles, you can choose the subcategory of science fiction (1,268 auctions), which breaks down into further subcategories for Babylon 5 (10), Buffy the Vampire Slayer (44), *Dr Who* (51), *Star Trek* (179), *Star Wars* (106), toys and games (741 – with more subcategories), *The X-Files* (112) and others (135). Many of these subcategories have the added bonus of direct links to Yahoo's main search engine, with ready-made searches a click away for matching chat rooms, message boards, clubs and related sites.

The rest

A1 Auctions Online At Bullnet   **www.bullnet.co.uk**
Bullnet are based in Brighton and sell a strange range of electronic devices. Primarily online retailers, their site features a special auctions page with a distinctly offbeat range of stock. A whole category is given over to surveillance equipment such as listening bugs at £27 ($40). Elsewhere are radios and transmitters, 'one million candle torches', all manner of computer accessories, plus

more conventional items such as Moulinex mixers and Philips Home Cinemas. Add VAT to the price of items you see on the site.

Amazon Auctions   **www.amazon.co.uk**

Amazon is considered one of the top three auction sites (along with Yahoo and eBay) in the USA, but it has made only a weak impression in the UK and it has some very low listings. In what looks like an attempt to disguise this, listings from its US sites appear on the UK site too. However, in one way, this could be an attraction: Amazon Auctions majors in books and CDs (like its main site) and these are all easily shipped so, in theory, the US listings are of interest. Amazon has installed a currency converter on its site for just such a purpose. If you want to see UK entries alone, the site offers a quick search option for this at the head of the page. Other useful functions let you search by start and end date as well as by price.

Amazon's book section is the best organised on the Net, with over twenty categories (including sections for signed and rare books) and has, generally, a better class of book than other sites. Your average Amazon user tends to be better educated than most and this tends to be reflected in the quality of listings.

Amazon is bolstered by merchant auctions with the odd glamour item such as one of Noel Gallagher's old electric guitars, a Smart car going for £1 and a signed photo of Muhammad Ali. Less appealing perhaps is its range of UK breaks, such as the offer of three nights in Llandudno for £80.

Another useful feature of the site is that if you are already registered with the Amazon online shop then you are automatically registered for its auctions too. Amazon's main shopping pages provide links straight to related auctions at Amazon, so a customer who found a book deleted on the main site might be tempted to trace the book on the relevant auction link. Amazon also provides an escrow service.

Aucland   www.aucland.co.uk

Aucland is a small (17,000 members) but attractive, well-laid-out site that makes it a favourite to survive any future clearout of the UK auction sector. Its biggest listings at present are for CDs and records, which hover around the 10,000 mark. Many of these listings appear to come from large dealers, such as the person selling a huge collection of Manchester United programmes in the sports section. The site is also a source of high-profile merchant auctions (e.g. ten multimedia notebooks at £600). Aucland has links to French, Italian and Spanish branches too.

Auction Town   www.auctiontown.co.uk

This dour, lo-fi site cheekily calls itself the UK premier online auction. It featured a disproportionate number of computer and electrical auctions for which there were few bidders. This seems largely the fault of some terminally slow links.

Auctionzone   www.auctionzone.co.uk

Designed like a computer circuit board, Auctionzone's site is appropriately for auctions of all things electronic, with computer products hogging the listings. Despite less than 100 auctions, the lots here are attracting a fair few bids.

Bidworth   www.bidworth.com

Nice site, good name, but only around 50 auctions for mainly computer products such as a Windows 2000 pack at £30 ($45) and PlayStation games at £27 ($40).

Buystuff   www.buystuff.co.uk

A mixture of around 100 classified adverts and auctions.

Cqout   www.cqout.com

Attractive well-laid-out site whose design is not a million miles away from that of eBay. Although only bobbing around the 1,500 listings mark, this site has some big-money backers and has been advertised regularly in the *Sunday Times* as the 'most trusted auction site'. The greatest activity here is for computers and software, followed by books, memorabilia and collectibles, with many categories dominated by a few large sellers. There are also a few obligatory merchant auctions dealing in products such as luxury watches. Cqout has its own escrow and shipping service, charged at 10% of the winning bid (minimum charge £5.00/$7.50).

Ebase5   www.ebase5.com

Fuelled by a loyal and unlikely band of computer geeks and Beanie collectors (some with feedback ratings of 100-plus), ebase5 claims to have shifted 60,000 items since starting in July 1999. There were less than a thousand auctions when we looked, 347 being computer related, 355 for Beanie Babies and 146 for Pokémon. If you know what a Teac CD-C8E CD autochanger and a Pentium 11/233 Mhz with heatsink and fan are, you will enjoy this site.

eBid   www.ebid.co.uk

eBid's early start in auctions in 1998 has allowed it to build up a small but steady membership. At present it has around 2,500 listings and a healthy level of bidding. Favourites on the site are Beanie Babies, computer hardware and software (where most of the bids are), electrical, Internet domain names and music. The site could be improved with faster links and bigger text.

Excite Auctions UK   http://auctions.excite.co.uk

A big player in the USA, Excite Auctions, along with its free consumer listings, was a welcome addition to the UK auction scene in the summer of 2000. In its first few weeks of UK trading it had clocked up 2,500 (mostly merchant) auctions, which represents only a fraction of the US site listings. Big names already signed up to the site include Network Q for second-hand Vauxhall cars, First Call Tickets and Butlins. The biggest listings were for merchant auctions of computers, DVDs and computer games.

Goricardo   www.goricardo.com

Goricardo have built up an enormous level of auctions, at around 100,000 items, through free listings and encouraging dealers to make bulk listings. However, there is a woeful lack of bidding activity. The largest category is music and the CD section has around 20,000 listings. The site is promoted through glamour auctions such as Spice Girl Emma Bunton's blue spangly minidress and Jensen Button's racing helmet. There are also bargains among its merchant auctions: Samsung Portable MP3 players, designer kettles, palm-sized PCs and food mixers have been known to appear in £1 auctions.

Loot   www.loot.com

Despite being one of the most primitive lo-fi sites around, Loot's local ads should prove a winning formula. Based around local papers, all adverts here can be searched by region; for example, there were 758 auctions in the south west, 262 in Scotland's Borders and Central regions, 230 in Liverpool and the Wirral, 191 in Tyneside, 197 in East Anglia and so on. Classified listings take up the lion's share with 146,055 ads, though the auctions are bubbling around the 10,000 mark at present. The lack of feedback ratings and category breakdowns have led to some low-quality listings, with poor descriptions, few photos and – surprise, surprise – by the looks of it, few bids.

Tiny Traders www.tinytraders.com

Tiny is best for its merchant auctions of electronic products, such as miniature Internet quick cams starting at £1. Most are sold by UK suppliers but there are a few from Europe too. At the back of the site there are a few C2C auctions hidden away.

Whatamibid www.whatamibid.com

Clear professional UK-based site with big ambitions. At present the auction categories are dominated by a few dealers with multiple auctions for categories such as stamps, CDs and holidays. The site actually bills itself as 'Europe's Premier Online Auction' and has a special currency converter to help but, as yet, most items are of English origin.

//EUROPE

Caraplazza www.caraplazza.com

General French site with some 2,000 items, big on computers (500), cars (400) and games consoles (242). Also property and a 'wanted' page, cutely named 'Je recherche'.

eBay Germany www.ebay.de

By the looks of it, eBay is number one in Germany with over 340,000 items on this site.

Eurobid www.eurobid.com

It makes a change to see a European site being run from Paris rather than London or the USA. Although open to the UK, France, Germany, Spain and Italy, Eurobid is dominated by French and Spanish auctions. Descriptions often come in two or more languages but, although English is favoured, some linguistic skill is needed to get the best from this site. Once the Euro is common-place this site should run much more smoothly; at present, home currencies are favoured. From 10,000 items this site features a large category for wines, among them a Château-Lafite Rothschild at £363.69 (594.55 Euros). Anomalies include a more relaxed Euro attitude to porn, with a large 'adult' category, and a CD section full of French pop music. The site has its own escrow service, for which the buyer pays the fee and the seller pays the shipping.

QXL **www.qxl.it**
This site accesses the whole of qxl.com but selects all the Italian items at the top of its listings.

Ricardo **www.ricardo.nl**
The Ricardo group took over the Netherlands' top auction site, veilng.com, to make this.

Denmark Yahoo Auctions	**http://dk.auctions.yahoo.com**
France Yahoo Auctions	**http://fr.auctions.yahoo.com**
Germany Yahoo Auctions	**http://de.auctions.yahoo.com**
Italy Yahoo Auctions	**http://it.auctions.yahoo.com**
Spain Yahoo Auctions	**http://es.auctions.yahoo.com**
Sweden Yahoo Auctions	**http://se.auctions.yahoo.com**

These are all European language versions of Yahoo.

//USA

Buying from the USA is a mixed experience. Some advertisers welcome 'international' bids for the greater chance it gives them of making a sale. Other advertisers, though, take a once-bitten-twice-shy approach after bad experiences of shipping abroad. Generally though, buying from the USA takes a little extra time and patience – and you must remember that there are certain cultural differences to overcome. For a fuller explanation of how to get the most from trading with the USA see Chapters 2 and 3.

Amazon Auctions　　　　　　www.auctions.amazon.com

Amazon came to auctions late, in April 1999, but with eight million customers using its main site it quickly established itself and is now the third biggest US auction site behind Yahoo and eBay. Like the UK site, its strengths are in books and CDs.

Auction Addict　　　　　　　www.auctionaddict.com

Slick site with fast links that has drawn in around 23,000 auctions on its no-fees-for-sellers policy. Merchant auctions dominate, with large listings for jewellery from Thailand. The listings are also strong on collectibles, coins, memorabilia and stamps.

Auctions　　　　　　　　　　www.auctions.com

Like an American QXL, this site of 24,000 auctions has many C2C auctions (big categories include US sports cards, comic cards and Beanie Babies), but its bargain merchant and glamour auctions lead the way on the home page (e.g. Alaskan pop star Jewel and Ringo Starr selling off autographed T-shirts and CDs for charity). Auctions has fast links and is affiliated with Freeserve in the UK.

Auction Sales　　　　　　　www.auction-sales.com

This slick and easy-to-use merchant site has been running since 1996 and offers bargains on computers, general electronics, mobile phone accessories, jewellery and watches. The biggest category – surprise, surprise – is for computers. Items you might not expect to find in the UK include a Barbie-branded inkjet printer in one of many auctions starting at $1. Many of the sales are Dutch auctions and the site also does many B2B auctions.

Auction Soup　　　　　　　www.auctionsoup.com

300 items, with large listings for musical instruments and Beanie Babies.

Bid   www.bid.com

Excellent and expanding merchant site that, for the time being, does not take international orders. Worth a look for its bargain basement, which stocks some wonderfully daft products such as voice-activated dog commanders, cats' cradles, world-time calculators and raft inflators. The site also has many 24-hour auctions and declining price auctions covering computer stuff, electronics, jewellery, home and sports.

Bidhit   www.bidhit.com

Bloke-orientated merchant site with bargains on binoculars and telescopes, mountain bikes, baseball memorabilia, spycams, walkie-talkies, hand-held organisers as well as the usual software, mobile phone, TV, audio and digital DVD systems. All auctions are 3–4 days long and finish every Monday and Thursday.

Bidnow   www.bidnow.com

A lovely glossy-looking site with a good name, lots of optimistic slogans, but only 200 items on the last look. Proof that even the USA has small sites too.

Bidzilla   www.bidzilla.com

Enormous name, little site. The 400 auctions here are strong on collectibles and computers.

Boxlot   www.boxlot.com

A high-profile merchant and C2C site aimed primarily at women. From 53,000 auctions there are large listings for kitchenware, clothes, dolls and figurines. The registration page is helpful for those logging on from abroad. Also bulletin boards and chat.

Buy Bid Win   www.buybidwin.com

It is worth a look just to see the psychedelic colour scheme on this site. Split into three sections for shopping, auctions and lucky number games – hence the site name – there are around 90,000 lots here, mostly from merchants; notable for a large collectibles section with a large advertising category full of Pepsi and Coca-Cola paraphernalia.

City Auction   **www.cityauction.com**

An enormous mix of 156,000 auctions and classified ads from both merchants and consumers. Part of the Fairmarket network, which means many of the same auctions you would find at Excite and MSN. This site is notable for its well-laid-out clothing and collectibles sections. These local auctions inspire greater trust.

Digiseller   **www.digiseller.com**

Seven hundred (mainly merchant) auctions from a site based in Florida.

eBay   **www.ebay.com**

eBay is so big that its search function is almost as rewarding as using Google. Put in any subject and the chances are that there will be something related to it in your search results. eBay started out as a collectibles site and that is still where its strengths are today with enormous listings for CDs, tapes and vinyl (250,000), books (240,000), autographs (41,000), coins (51,000), stamps (95,000), advertising (100,000), Pez (2,450), Barbie dolls (18,000), general dolls (45,000), trolls (946), *Dr Who* (1,220), *Star Wars* (4,335), *Star Trek* (4,531), snowdomes (518), die-cast toys (81,738) and antiques and art (11,442). A visit to eBay can be an education too. There is a whole subcategory for scripophily, the name given to the dubious hobby of collecting old stock bonds; meanwhile, exonumia turns out to be a category for the collection of elongated coins and breyer the group name for model horses. If there is a weakness in the listings, it is that the site cannot be maintained as rigorously as some of the better specialist sites, thus you end up with some categories like art posters containing an ad for a Limp Bizkit poster. There can be problems for the seller too; in some of the larger collectible categories it is hard to make an item stand out from the crowd. Still, eBay should be most auction users' first point of call.

Excite Auctions   www.auctions.excite.com

Excite in the USA is the biggest of all the merchant auction sites, with 145,000 listings. Although it has free C2C listings too, these tend to get lost among a swathe of auctions from dealers who pack category headings such as computers and software (34,000 auctions) and jewellery (20,000 auctions). For each category dominated by the merchants you tend to get endless lists of similar items, such as bracelets or CD-ROMs, which makes browsing monotonous. Furthermore, many of these retailers seem to be exempt from feedback ratings. Collectibles, at 30,000 listings, is more consumer driven, though this site is very poor for music listings. Note around half the merchants on this site do not ship to the UK.

First Auction   www.firstauction.com

A women-orientated merchant site that at present limits itself to shipping in the USA only. Sticking to only a handful of select items per category, it covers electronics, home furnishings, houseware and gourmet, collectibles and gifts, clothes, health and beauty, gold and silver.

Gold's Auction   www.goldsauctions.com

A high-profile US site, with mainly C2C auctions that surprisingly had only a rather sickly 10,000 items on it. No particular categories stand out as being large. Fast links but low bid activity.

Lycos   http://Auctions.lycos.com
Auctions   http://auction.msn.com

Not surprisingly for an auction run by Microsoft, software makes up the biggest category here, with 25,000 listings. What is surprising, though, is the number of dodgy items posted to the site, such as spy software 'to help you spy on your neighbours' or software to eliminate bad credit ratings. Jewellery, with 18,000 auctions (15,000 diamond rings!), is the next biggest category, which, like software, is dominated by merchant auctions. There are also large listings for CDs and vinyl on this large but characterless site.

Makeusanoffer www.makeusanoffer.com

This site does not ship internationally at present, but it's worth a browse to see one of the most unusual auction gimmicks – Chester, an animated auction puppet who looks like Colonel Sanders of Kentucky Fried Chicken fame. The site works by you finding an item and then making what you think is a reasonable offer. Make an offer too low and Chester will reply with something like 'Make me a more reasonable offer'. Chester of course is pre-programmed with what the site thinks is a reasonable price; once you have reached that happy medium then the item is yours instantly, you do not have to compete with anyone else. All goods are surplus stock bought up by the site.

Nu Auction www.nuauction.com

Part of the Fairmarket auction group, this site has the usual enormous listings for computer and jewellery merchant auctions, plus listings for 20,000 collectibles, 13,000 toys and 6,000 Beanie Babies.

Pawn Shop Bargains www.pawnshopbargains.com

Not a real pawnshop – that bit is just to gain your attention for what is yet another merchant auction site. Of interest here is the religious section with kitsch classics such as a Jesus nightlight at $8.

Popula www.popula.com

'You have arrived at the auction with soul' announces the home page of Popula, one of the most unique auction sites in the USA. Popula takes a witty and irreverent stance on auctions and is aimed at arty US liberals. A stylishly designed site has around 1,000 listings of C2C auctions, big on Hollywood (anything film related), books, music, vintage/designer wear, erotica and home. Also worth checking out for one of the best auction forum pages in existence, found on the 'Vox Pop' link – members here discuss anything from auction tips, to life, to the worst films ever made.

Rocket 8   **www.rocket8.com**
Contrived, global site aimed at teenagers. Rocket 8 awards auction points to those who shop at the featured advertisers, which can then be used to bid on items such as Ginza toys, Sega consoles and games, mobile phones, snowboard and skate wear, Diesel, GAP and DKNY clothes. A bit too complicated to work, but you never know.

321Gone   **www.321gone.com**
Nice site with 2,000 items and very good listings for dolls, figurines, games and toys and collectibles.

Webswap   **www.webswap.com**
Another niche market beyond the realms of eBay. At this general US site, under each category there is a page for swaps and a page for 'wants'. Find an item you like and then approach the buyer with your swaps lists and see if you can find an agreement. If you have nothing worth swapping then make them a bid in cash. Popular site items are CDs (12,352), electronic games (13,172), Beanies (8,433), books (12,656) and clothing and accessories (7,739).

What The Heck Is That   **www.whattheheckisthat.com**
Nice name and a good introduction, which announces it is 'Where the unusual is usual'. Sadly a rather bland site of only 150 items, 77 of which were comics.

Yahoo Auctions   **www.auctions.yahoo.com**

Yahoo's total of two million auctions are snapping at the heels of eBay's domination of the auction market, but when you look at the quality of the auctions these numbers pale. Sports cards (400,000) make up the biggest category, dealers in these cards taking advantage of the site's bulk loading device that allows individuals to post multiple items. Elsewhere, big categories (such as jewellery, with 139,000 auctions) come mostly from merchants. What quality there is on the site can be found in the other bid listings for antiques and collectibles (381,646 auctions), Beanies (33,000), CDs (32,000), vinyl (35,000), books (171,000), Pokémon cards (134,000) and software items (30,000). The large numbers of pages on these listings make it advisable to always use the search function first.

//REST OF THE WORLD

The best

Sold   **www.sold.com.au**

A wide and often surprising range of auctions with 28,000 lots. Among the featured auctions was a Paul Cézanne etching, while among the featured categories are all things connected to the Sydney 2000 Olympics. Also good for Aussie wines, stamps, rock and Aboriginal art.

The rest

eBay Australia   **www.ebay.com.au**

At 28,000 auctions, eBay Australia is head to head with the Sold site (above); its listings are dominated by the collectibles section (at 11,031) and books, music and films (at 7,146).

eBay Canada   http://pages.ca.ebay.com
The categories covering collectibles and books, music and films comprise half of the 205,000 items listed here.

eBay Japan   www.ebayjapan.co.jp
eBay's Japanese site.

Hong Kong Yahoo Auctions   www.hk.auctions.yahoo.com
Under the hammer in Cantonese.

Korea Yahoo Auctions   www.kr.auctions.yahoo.com
Yahoo! Korea enters the auction fray.

MercadoLibreUSA   www.mercadolibreusa.com
Large site covering Argentina, Brazil, Chile, Columbia, Spain, USA, Mexico, Uruguay and Venezuela.

Nifty   http://seri.nifty.com
Lively Japanese site.

Subasta   www.subasta.com
From Tijuana down to Tierra del Fuego, this Spanish-language site (based in Florida) caters for the whole of Latin America.

Surfingbananas   www.surfingbananas.com
A collection of auctions for Far East countries; its pages for Singapore, Malaysia and the Philippines are all in English.

Taiwan Yahoo Auctions   www.tw.auctions.yahoo.com
Made in Taiwan.

Trade Me   www.trademe.co.nz
Two and a half thousand auctions but no one strong area of activity at this Kiwi site that has its own escrow service, message board, cafe and Internet news service.

7//GENERAL DIRECTORY

The following sites represent the best the Net has to offer in online auctions; occasionally, though, where a site does not cater for those in the UK, we have left it out. The quality of these sites varies in the same way as all sites do on the Net: some use state-of-the-art software and are multinational corporations; some are one-man operations without any auction software, merely taking email bids. Ironically, these one-man operations with minimal overheads will probably be around longer than some of the other, larger sites that are trying to compete with eBay. If you think some of these smaller sites are pretty minimal, you would be right, but if you think you can do better, well, why not start your own?

//ANTIQUES AND GENERAL COLLECTIBLES

Commodities that are rare, limited or one of a kind benefit the most from online auctions. For the sellers they provide a chance to gain a true national market value, where previously they had to accept the value reached in restricted local markets. For the buyers too they are a boon: no longer do they have to constantly browse the same local shops or make long, possibly fruitless, expeditions to other towns or cities. The increased ease of trade for such antiques and collectibles should also encourage a greater volume of turnover in trade. This is especially so for small and sturdy items that are easily shipped, but the sales of grandfather clocks and four-poster beds will benefit less. In the USA many dealers now derive most of their income from sales made at eBay.

Auctions also open up the possibilities of foreign trade and, for many UK sellers of antiques, the prices US buyers are willing to pay may be far greater than the going rates at home.

When browsing the following sites do not forget that often the best selections of collectibles are to be found at eBay. In the UK, QXL have recently moved into the area of antiques, appointing Hugh Scully from the BBC's *Antiques Roadshow* to provide onsite valuations.

The best

eBay Great Collections   www.ebaygreatcollections.com

Another bright idea from eBay, who are muscling into the posh end of the auction market with this special site for antiques, art and collectibles. All auctions come from specialist dealers or real-time auction houses (notably Butterfields). Each section is presented gallery-style, with the photos already downloaded, making it great to browse. The jewellery and fine art sections are very strong and other notable categories are for Asian art, dolls and toys, rock memorabilia and native and tribal art. Just like the main eBay site, all dealers can be given feedback. This site is unique in that all items here carry a guarantee.

Icollector   www.icollector.com

Like an auction of surplus stock from the British Museum, the quality and range at this site is fantastic. You can find anything from an ancient Inca cloth to a Picasso lithograph, a Dali etching or a print by De Kooning. On the Net since 1994, Icollector has built up a big reputation and yet, unlike some of the other top sites, it never tries to look posh or intimidating. Along with a wide range of art and antiques you will also find auctions for cigars, film, rock and pop memorabilia, sporting memorabilia and wines. The site also gives news of real-time auctions, dealer contacts worldwide, an art price guide and much more. Icollector insures all items up to the value of $50,000 (£33,000).

Nicebid   www.nicebid.com

Nidebid is a general site that has become a forum for the sale of thousands of vintage US TV and film magazines, with a heavy bias to the 1950s and 1960s. For the Audrey Hepburn, Marylin Monroe and Frank Sinatra completists out there, this is a gold mine, but some of the mags look on the dull side. Elsewhere are historical newspapers and magazines for fashion, sci-fi and cars.

Pottery Auction   www.potteryauction.com

Neatly arranged, this US site allows easy browsing among an amazing 50 categories of pottery, with headings such as American Art, Hull, Japanese, Porcelain, Royal Doulton and Utilitarian. Prices are on the low side, suggesting not all items are of the highest quality, with many bids starting as low as $1. Site extras include chat and forum pages, news, feature articles, restoration tips, fake alert pages and book lists.

Ruby Lane   www.rubylane.com

Ruby Lane offers two services: a search on antiques at auction sites across the web and a host site for 500 small dealers worldwide (i.e. dealers too small to have their own auction sites). The popularity of this service grew to such a level that it was rumoured that eBay, seriously worried by Ruby Lane's success, pulled its links from this site in 1999. However, the site still boasts links to 1,500,000 items at auction, with its strength lying in antiques rather than art or collectibles.

Running Rabbit Productions   www.runningrabbit.com

Friendly, easy-to-use site from Tennessee, USA, which features lots of beautifully photographed marbles, all of which are sold direct from the site, which at present only takes email bids.

Sothebys Amazon   http://sothebys.amazon.com

This site is a joy, a brilliant collaboration between Sothebys and Amazon offering a truly classy collection of affordable antiques, art and a very populist range of collectibles and memorabilia. The 4,500 items listed here all come from professional dealers, ensuring a level of quality (though perhaps not so many bargains) you would not find at eBay. The site has a fun layout with great photos, is great for browsing and is clearly aimed at as wide an audience as possible. Featured auctions included detective novels, a framed autograph of all four Beatles, rare sports programmes and a Roman ring. Shipping and payment are arranged for you via the Amazon site, but in return you pay a 10% buyer's fee. Each item comes with a property certificate and an authenticity guarantee.

The rest

ACargo   www.acargo.com

Some lovely Marc Chagall and Joan Miró prints and lithographs were the star attractions on last viewing at this quality Washington DC-based site whose main categories are paintings, art glass, silver, militaria and pottery. All transactions are direct with the site, which also provides a guarantee for each item. Sadly not at present selling internationally.

Action Figure Auctions   www.actionfigureauctions.com

Lots of plastic and cheap-looking toys on this US site, most of which seem to be spin-offs of recent films (e.g. *Austin Powers*, *Danger Girl*, *Spawn* and the re-released *Yellow Submarine*). For some reason, the site also carries Ozzy Osbourne dolls.

Acubid   www.acubid.com

A US site run 'by collectors for collectors' with some 500 lots, the biggest for toys and antiques.

Allegria   www.allegria.co.uk

Tiny UK arts and crafts site that amusingly titles itself the 'UK's premier online market for quality arts and crafts'. Has links to around ten artists and shops, which also sell the products at fixed prices. Items include porcelain, glass, pottery and sculptures.

Antique-Trails   www.antique-trails.com

Pretty Pre-Raphaelite-decorated site from the USA, selling anything from art to trading cards, with good sections for pottery and glassware. All transactions are direct with the site.

The Auction Channel   www.theauctionchannel.com

If you are too busy to jet across the world to place your bid on that $50 million Van Gogh then this site will let you take part. The Auction Channel sets up live Internet connections to auction houses such as Phillips, Bonhams, Christies and more. Recent auctions included boxing memorabilia, rugs, classic cars and decorative arts. Specialities are the property auctions via London-based Allsop & Co, wine auctions with Morrell & Co in New York and watches via Antiquorum.com in Geneva. Tracking an auction, which might be over in minutes, while staring at your screen is not an easy process, so this site has a practice simulator to allow you to adjust to the pace of the bidding. Terms of payment apply to each specific auction house.

Auction Club   www.auctionclub.com

All things 'collectible' are listed on this 500-item US site, including big categories for advertising, comic books and Pez.

Auction Port   www.auctionport.com

Small US antiques and collectibles site with a few auctions for dolls and figurines, jewellery, timepieces, pottery and porcelain.

Auctions Unlimited   www.auctions-unlimited.com

Cheap prices from an attractive 150-item range of twentieth-century US curios such as bears, puzzles, ornaments and figurines, all sold direct from a site based in New York. 1930s – 1950s items are a speciality.

Biddingtons   www.biddingtons.com

Despite its drab old-fashioned site design, this US site is a source of some quality art and antiques. Strongest on paintings, which make up 250 of its 400 auctions, most items are provided by small galleries and professional dealers. Useful extras include occasional essays on categories or artists to help the buyer. The site also operates an escrow service, sending out items when payment is received and providing the buyer with a seven-day approval period.

Cartamania   www.geocities.com/~cartamania

Italian comics, postcards, movie posters, drawings and Disneyania, all lovingly laid out on this site which holds real-time auctions that accept e-mail bids.

Collectex   www.collectex.com

Proof that people will collect anything, this US general collectors' site is taken up with auctions of Anheuser-Busch steins, which, for the uninitiated, are decorative German beer mugs.

Collectors Universe   www.collectorsauction.com

A good collective site of US dealers who specialise in coins, autographs, stamps and single and LP records. Some of the dealers sell at fixed prices and some auction their items.

Crystal-Auction   www.crystal-auction.com

Specialists in Swarovski crystal glass, which comes in the shapes and forms of drinking glasses, ornaments and clocks. The site appears to have a co-brand deal with eBay, judging by the look of its auction software.

Crystal Maze www.crystalmaze.co.uk
An excellent example of how to run an amateur auction site. A solo dealer here runs one-off auctions every few months for zeolite and fluorite crystals. For the last auction most lots sold at prices between £3 ($5) and £10 ($16.50).

e hammer www.ehammer.com
This is the online offshoot of a New York auction house that majors in US antiques but also has categories for Asian art, prints, comic books, photography, porcelain, toys, jewellery and Native American art. If you are in New York you can drop by to view the 700 items on sale.

Gem Traders www.gemtraders.com
A fun, collective site of gem dealers who both sell and auction their stock of mostly unmounted stones and occasional jewellery, categorised by name from amethysts to turquoise.

Golden Age Antiquities www.goldnage.
and Collectibles com
This US site promises much with an eccentric opening page, which looks as if it is floating on clouds. However, the 1,000-plus auctions are nothing unusual, with large listings for jewellery, pottery, glass and porcelain.

Greg Manning www.gregmanning.com
A high-profile US dealer who has a small but high-quality selection of movie posters, lobby stills, comics and stamps. 'Auctions by trusted collectors', says the site.

Ibidlive   www.ibidlive.com

'Not physically present at auctions but still want to bid?' is the tag line of this impressive site, now part-owned by QXL, which allows you to place live Internet bids to real-time auctions worldwide. Of the six pending auctions, two were for property in London and one each was for art in Switzerland, Austria, Germany and France, the last one featuring such names as Emil Nolde, Max Ernst, Kandinsky and Maurice Utrillo. Future auctions included those for antiques, bankrupt stock, wines, collectibles and government stock. Based in Amsterdam, this site lists links to auction houses throughout Europe, Australia and the USA. On site is an archive giving past auction results.

Internet Auction Gallery   www.intag.net

Small collection of upmarket Californian antiques dealers who have a handful of superb items on sale.

Jewel Net Auctions   www.jewelnetauctions.net

Only 200 auctions here but a great range, from a Ceylon sapphire stone at $6,000 (about £4,000) down to a $12.90 (£8.50) necklace. The main categories are for antique, costume, unmounted, diamond and gold jewellery. A neat little site but not a lot of bids.

Just Beads   www.justbeads.com

You would not have guessed that beads could be so popular. This ambitious site provides not only auctions but also an amazing range of bead chat, bead forums, upcoming events, notices, featured artists pages and bead tips – no doubt this is all going to make someone very happy. Its auction listings stay around the 600 mark under the categories of stones and cameos, beaded jewellery, books, buttons and beaded artwork.

Just Glass   www.justglass.com

Brilliantly organised US site with 500 lots covering 28 categories of glassware including art glass, bottles, paperweights, stained glass and Vaseline glass. The prices look fairly low, though some items are for fixed-price sale. Site extras include an online bookstore, magazine, dealer contacts and library.

Madelena Antiques   www.madelenaantiques.com

A model example of how to link a homepage to eBay. At the above address you learn about the dealer and the items for sale, but click to bid and you are taken through to eBay. Madelena Antiques, although UK based, has smartly catered for the US market by putting its prices in dollars and, judging by the bidding for its auctions, it does very well. The categories here are for green Majolica (leafy plates), Majolica (leafy but less green), Staffordshire figurines and jewellery (mainly rings).

Marble Collecting.com   www.blocksite.com

This large site, with its numerous links to marble auctions, chat rooms, links, shopping, guides, books and bulletin boards, appears not to have hosted any auctions since December 1999, but it might be worth checking out.

Modern Auction   www.modernauction.com

Slickly designed site for lovers of twentieth-century furniture and accessories, covering everything from art nouveau up to modern repro, with art deco and 60s classics along the way. Despite its lovely design, this site at present looks very empty with only twelve items, most of them lamps ($100-500/£66-330) in the 50s category.

Nickleby's   www.nicklebys.com

Auction house from Denver, Colorado, which has gone successfully online with its classy collection of lots covering antiques, art, posters and collectibles. The site also carries a unique 'south western' category, which features a mix of Red Indian and Mexican art. Top items included a Salvador Dali woodcut and lithographs from Marc Chagall and Toulouse Lautrec. Biographies are also listed for all artists.

Old Marbles   www.oldmarbles.com

The auctions on this site are linked to eBay and have earned a feedback rating there of over 300. This home site also features marble price guides, reference books, accessories and news.

Online Poster Auction   www.onlineposterauction.com

A grand name for a collection of posters sold by a dealer based in Florida who offers Maître de L'Affiche Parisian posters dating from 1890-1910, which have an art nouveau style, European advertising posters from the twentieth century and European movie posters from the same era. Prices range from $70 (£46) upwards. All posters, judging by their attractiveness, have been wisely chosen.

Pacific Glass Auctions   www.pacglass.com

Claiming to be the largest antique bottle auction house on the Net, this site features some beautiful examples, but the auctions are one-off events for which, tiresomely, catalogues must be ordered before bids can be submitted by email.

Phillips Auctioneers   www.phillips-auctions.com/uk

Phillips, who deal in anything from aircraft to 'writing equipment', are presently letting you place email bids on their real-time auctions. They are also dipping a toe into the online auction market with Internet-only auctions of rare and fine wines.

Pinbacks   www.pinbacks.com

A fair collection of badges, which go by the name of pinbacks in the USA. The largest selection is of US presidential election badges for the likes of Lyndon Johnson and Richard Nixon.

Playle's Online Auctions www.playle.com

A collective site for several US dealers, the biggest of whom has a 4,000-plus collection of postcards ranging from travel scenes to erotica and Hollywood stars. Another dealer has a small but select range of vintage jewellery, but do not bother with the lame CDs page.

Serious Collector www.seriouscollector.com

A large and fascinating site with a unique and at times odd range of US collectibles. Its lots originate from an approved list of 180 specialist dealers, some of who sell their stock at fixed prices. Antiques, curios, memorabilia and art are what it does best, with a large category for antique advertising paraphernalia including the unusual (and presumably of sentimental value for someone) tin of 1950s 'Sheik Condoms' at $195 (£130).

Speedbid www.speedbid.com

Speedbid started life as a general site but has become a well-established UK venue for British militaria. The 200-plus auctions are mainly for medals but also feature books, badges, buttons, magazines and great curiosities like air-raid-shelter tickets. Judging by the high feedback ratings of many of the dealers, this site does a healthy trade.

Teletrade Auctions www.teletrade.com

Uninformative site with links to real-time auctions in New York, where you will find a quality selection of coins and diamonds.

The Trade Card Place www.tradecards.com

Loving, attractive site for those into the trade cards that were used to advertise American goods and services in the late 1800s.

Utopia's Treasures www.utauction.com

A 500-item general site big on 1920s-1950s collectibles, with big entries for all things Bakelite, toys such as Buck Rogers, 1930s space soldiers and strange categories like tobacciana, plus loads of those sort of awful mementoes you buy on holiday from gift shops (but older).

Vintage Film Posters   www.vintagefilmposters.com

Ohio-based real-time auction house with one-off enormous film poster auctions for which online bids can be placed. Among a host of Hollywood films from 1910 to the 1980s, the pick of the crop were original posters for Hitchcock's *Vertigo* (about $2,500/£1,650), *Bonnie and Clyde* (about $300/£200) and *The Wizard of Oz* (about $3,200/£2,100). Add a 15% purchase charge to the prices of the posters, which are all graded by the site.

West 10   www.west10.com

Antiques, art, memorabilia from UK-based dealers and artists – paintings priced between £400 ($660) and £800 ($1,330). From 300 listings there is a mixture of fixed-price sales and auctions. The site ran a recent special Armani auction to raise money for the London Lighthouse project. Also has news, feature articles, chat rooms, forum pages and links.

//ART

Like the market for antiques, online auctions have opened up an enormous opportunity for increased trade, buyer choice and higher prices for rare items. Occasionally for impoverished artists too, they have opened up increased opportunities to sell their work.

The real coming of age for art online auctions came when eBay sold a Van Gogh for $5 million (£3.3 million). Such events brought the previously reticent big art auction houses into the market quickly to catch up.

Online auctions, by their nature, cannot be too snooty, though some of the more established auction houses have tried to maintain their rarefied atmosphere through some laughably intimidating sites. Such institutions, though, still carry with them the suspicion that people would only buy online once they have seen the real thing. At present many of the traditional auction houses favour online auctions of prints and photographs, which can be well represented when viewed online. There are accusations too that such sites are only selling online what has not sold through traditional methods. More darkly, there are reports of some American sites selling fake Chagall prints.

Art Conte   www.artconte.com

Small London-based site for Russian artists' sculptures, paintings, conceptual art, photography, computer art and drawings priced in US dollars. A confusing site that suffered from several broken links.

Art London   www.artlondon.com

A collective site for London-based dealers in antiques and art, all with some Asian or East European link. The homepage provides straightforward sales, though an auction link takes you through to auctions for new and affordable representational paintings, nearly all having some Russian theme.

Art Net   www.artnet.com

Big general US art site that at present is only putting a toe in the water of online auctions, sticking mainly to prints, photography and vintage posters. Best items on site were a 1959 Picasso linoleum print at an estimated $28,000 (£18,500) and an Andy Warhol screenprint of The Scream at an estimated $15,000 (£10,000). Such big items all come with a long, wordy description and a comparative history of bids for similar items on the site.

Buyers are charged a 10% premium for which the site provides both shipping and an escrow service. Extras are links to 700 galleries worldwide, a news service, feature articles and a database of 1.8 million works.

Art Online   www.myartonline.com

Large US site that suffers some awful item descriptions and, mysteriously, does not list its credentials, merely saying it is staffed by 'professionals'. Features 900-plus lots (some for sale, some for auction) including Russian Icons at $1,395 (£925), Manet and Chagall etchings at $1,250 (£825), rare posters, ceramics, pottery and glass. The site offers an escrow service, links to top art galleries, resource and advice pages, news, biographies and price guides.

Bonhams   www.bonhams.com

This traditional auction house started its online auctions in the summer of 2000. As well as providing links to its real-time auctions, Bonhams held three separate online auctions, one for vintage wines, one for classic twentieth-century furniture and another for reproduction architecture. All these auction lots were viewable at Bonhams' six British showrooms. Their real-time auctions at present cover everything from paintings and jewellery to sports and pop memorabilia.

Butterfields   www.butterfields.com

Butterfields, one of the USA's oldest auction houses, was recently acquired by eBay to lend some credibility to its ventures in the quality art and antiques market. Butterfields itself carries on its traditional real-time auctions for which online bids can be made. Five to ten auctions take place a month, covering a wide range of art and antiques, memorabilia, natural history and wines. The winning bidders pay a hefty 15% premium.

Gavelnet   www.gavelnet.com

Wary that people will not buy antiques or art they cannot see in person, Gavelnet sticks to colourful items that show up well on the Net. The site claims only to work with 'respected galleries and dealers' and offers 10–30 items in each category from its range of prints, ceramics and glass, books, maps, jewellery, watches, entertainment memorabilia, sports, autographs and posters. A notable item on the site was a black cardigan ($600-1200/£400-800 estimate) worn by Winona Ryder in the film *Girl Interrupted*. All payment is direct to Gavelnet, which offers a guarantee on each item and will arrange shipping too, for which it charges a 10% buyer's premium.

London Art   www.londonart.co.uk

Contemporary art from London-based galleries goes at auction from prices between £500 ($830) and £1,500 ($2,500). At present only three artists' work is available for auction at any one time. This work is, by modern art standards, colourful, attractive and generally easy on the eye.

Refocus-Now   www.refocus-now.co.uk

Weird London-based site whose homepage describes itself as an art exchange for new media, but click on the link 'HyperSpace' and you go through to a page auctioning abstract and representational 'Cyber' art made on computers.

Sothebys   www.sothebys.com

Relatively late in joining the online auction set, Sothebys decided to offer something really special on its arrival and is rumoured to have spent £25 million ($41.5 million) perfecting its site. The result is one of the poshest, most foreboding sites on the Net, no doubt to inspire the trust of its rich and powerful clients. There is nothing downmarket here, the lots sticking to quality art and antiques. The jewellery page is typical, with such lovely items as an unmounted yellow 0.6-carat diamond with a reserve of £1,250 ($2,100). Everything is beautifully photographed and presented. At present, though, the site has gone more for novelty than for famous works of art, hence an auction for the original menu from the *Titanic*, the most famous artist represented being Georges Seurat. Sothebys offers buyers a three-year authenticity guarantee and refunds if the item purchased turns out to be 'materially different' to its description on the site. An online guide gives useful tips to buyers, who on winning an auction must pay a 10% buyer's premium.

Ukiyo-e World   **www.ukiyo-e-world.com**
Hundreds of lovely Japanese woodprints from the early nineteenth century to the modern day are available at this site based in Munich, which provides much background information on the history of each print. Auctions are held once a month at EST (New York time) with all transactions taking place direct with the site, which charges a 15% buyer's premium.

Whytes   **www.whytes.ie**
Dublin-based auctioneers since 1785, Whytes hold real-time auctions for which they accept email bids. All items from categories such as fine art, books, stamps, coins, militaria, toys, maps, photos and sports memorabilia have a strong Irish bias and can be viewed online.

//AUTOGRAPHS

Buying autographs has its good and bad sides: while they are easily displayed on screen and easily shipped, they are also a popular item among fraudsters. In the USA, and because of this, the law states that all autographs must come with a certificate of authenticity.

The best

Beverley Hills Charity Auction   www.bhauction.com

Probably the best-connected auction site on the Net, the people at Beverley Hills can auction you new, signed photos of Warren Beatty, Jack Nicholson, Robert De Niro, Sharon Stone, Kim Basinger, George Clooney, Mike Myers as Austin Powers, Jackie Chan, Richard Gere and Cindy Crawford (together) and more, with prices from $150 (£100) to $300 (£200). Each photo is suitably flattering and comes with a beautiful flourishing signature. The proceeds go to American Air Rescue, the Dana-Farber cancer institute and butterfly conservation! There is also some top US sports memorabilia for sale here too.

The rest

Autograph Auction   www.autographauction.com

'The only place that you need to look for the greatest deals in the autograph industry' is the grand claim of this site, which only had 67 auctions of note, mainly for Hollywood actors and actresses (e.g. a Johnny Depp autograph selling at $29/£19 and Kevin Costner at $40/£26.50).

Gallery Of History   www.galleryofhistory.com

Thomas Jefferson, Albert Einstein and Bill Gates are the sorts of names you would expect to find at this rather studious, badly designed site that is big on figures from US history, science and politics and claims a stock of 184,000 autographs. All payment goes to the site, which charges an extra 15% buyer's premium. Also framing services and a guarantee of authenticity.

//BEANIE BABIES

Nothing on online auctions has inspired such passion and sales as that of Beanie Babies. If you are feeling a little left out of this craze and you are wondering just what a Beanie Baby is, visit the lushly coloured manufacturer's site at **www.ty.com**, which has a gallery of every Beanie ever made. In effect they are stuffed toys with cute and original names, and mainly come in the shape of bears, but also as cats, dogs, walruses, etc. When demand drops off for one of these Beanies then Ty halts production, making each bear's second-hand value soar, depending, that is, on how desirable the bear is. Pandemonium was caused recently when Ty introduced a bear only available in Japan, the cherry-blossom-coloured Sakura Beanie Baby. These were brought over to the USA by collectors and did a roaring trade on online auction sites.

When looking at Beanies at auction listings you will notice that many are described as 'retired'; these are the most valuable bears and the ones that have had their production run ended.

If you think this is all a little strange and far-fetched then you would be right, but many bears seem to be bought with the sole purpose of trading them on. The most attractive way you can describe a Beanie is to say that it is still sealed within its plastic wrapper with the original tags attached. Proof of just how weird the Beanie phenomenon can get is at **www.metaexchange.com**, a stock exchange for Beanie Babies. As the following small selection of Beanie sites suggests, the best places to look for Beanies are at Yahoo and eBay.

Beanie Nation   **www.beanienation.com**

Enormous and easy-to-use US site (with over 3,000 auctions of Beanies) that has an awesome range of extras such as Beanie news pages, message boards, reports on bad traders, shops, games, discussion pages, links, searches and a list of top searches.

Collecting Nation   www.collectingnation.com

Hosts large 'Beanie Nation' page with regular auctions of around 2,500 Beanies. Here you will also find Beanie News, chat and links.

Lemon Lainey Babies   www.lemonlaineydesign.com

The leading British Beanie Baby site has around 50 'retired' bears for auction, all of which appear to be owned by the site, which photographs and grades each bear. Good extras are a Beanie Baby gallery, a past auction winners' table, which acts as a price guide, a guest book for Beanie Baby contacts, a news page and a shop. At the last time of looking, the auctions seemed to have closed.

//BIKES

Bidabike   www.bidabike.com

UK site with lots of bargain merchant auctions for what appear to be surplus stock bikes. From over 300 listings there are big categories for mountain bikes (from £140/$232) and BMX bikes (from £80/$133) plus smaller ones for children's and women's bikes. The site also provides lots of bike links and news and charges £10–15 for UK delivery. The site at present is spoiled by poor navigation and broken links to images, which do not inspire trust.

//BUSINESS

Living down to expectations, most business sites are deathly dull and lacking good graphics, passion and character. It also has to be said that the British sites are some of the worst culprits. Things can only get better.

eBay UK   www.ebay.co.uk

eBay's professional, trustworthy auction services are welcome on the dull UK business auction scene. At present you can find their B2B auctions on the eBay UK homepage under the link 'The small business exchange'. Items are listed in the same way as the rest of the site but are chosen for this special page for their perceived usefulness to small businesses. Particularly strong on computer items such as laptops, systems and services, there are also headings for restaurants, industrial, hardware supplies and farm equipment.

Freemarkets Asset   www.assetauctions.
Exchange   freemarkets.com

BP Amoco and SmithKline Beecham have been signed up for this worldwide site with big ambitions and large press exposure. The emphasis is on industrial plant and machinery, for example, a hydraulic surface grinder at $2,300 (£1,500). To place a bid you must call the site, which also arranges asset exchanges and straight purchases.

Import Quote   www.importquote.com

An ambitious UK reverse auction site that seeks to match importers and exporters worldwide. It works by the importer placing an advert on the site and then waiting for exporters and manufacturers to offer tenders to match the bid. This service cannot be browsed without first registering, which costs $25 (£16.50) for six months' access.

Lowestbid Reverse Auctions   www.lowestbid.co.uk

One of the best UK business sites around lets companies or organisations put up jobs for tender. Each advert states a top price and companies log on to try to offer a competing (usually lower) price.

The contracts range from £2 million ($3.3 million) for laying cables and accessories to £800 ($1,300) offered for supplying 250 tons of sunflower oil. Adverts can be put under the categories of agriculture, building, engineering, resources and mining, vehicles and miscellaneous.

Trade Out   www.tradeout.com

It is Trade Out's boast that it is the 'worlds leading online surplus market place' and, with its excellent 4,500 listings, this cannot be far wrong. Goods range from a consignment of 100,000 German stainless steel knives to a flatbed-trailer truck. Although US-based, there are auctions advertised here from around the world and you can search the site by country alone. The main site categories are for clothing, computers, food, drinks, health and beauty, household, commercial transportation and power and utility equipment. Adverts are a mix of straight sales and auctions.

The rest

Able Auctions   www.ableauctions.com

Characterless US site with industrial clearance auctions such as contents of restaurants, factories and offices. Buyers are charged a 7–10% premium.

Bid Business   www.bidbusiness.co.uk

Ambitious site that aims to create a UK market place for business products and services that covers every sector from agriculture to packaging and from advertising to telecommunications. Very little activity here at the moment though.

Business Auctions   www.business-auctions.com

Up-and-running UK site whose 60-plus auctions vary from a Ferranti generator thermometer from a disused power station at

£10,000 ($16,500) to a large collection of onsite 'director'-style chairs. The main categories are assets, computing, leisure, medical, office, power station equipment and timber.

Business 2 Business Rover   www.b2brover.com
Comprehensive search site for US-orientated B2B auction sites.

Cyberswap   www.cyberswap.com
Uninformative US site that mixes B2B and C2C auctions, all hosted at eBay.

e-steel   www.e-steel.com
Worldwide site for the selling of newly made steel.

Farm Bid   www.farmbid.com
No new combine harvesters but lots of second-hand ones, as well as tractors, hay bailers and bulls on this large communal-style US site.

GPbid   www.gpbid.com
This German B2B site comes in English but rigid, unhelpful site navigation means you must register before you can browse – wonder how many lose interest at this stage?

Lot 1   www.lot1.com
Reconditioned and refurbished second-hand computer equipment from this site based in Dumfries, Scotland. Features over 300 lots for hard drives, monitors, systems, laptops, PC components and telecom equipment. Shame they had to colour this site so grey.

Metal Site   www.metalsite.com
Top US site for those buying and selling steel.

Nippon Trading Co Ltd   www.nitr.co.jp
Used construction vehicles from Japan for export, such as loaders, graders, excavators, rollers, cranes, tractors and so on.

Oracle Exchange   www.oraclexchange.com

Oracle has made its boss Larry Ellison one of the richest men in the world, which is an idea of how prestigious this site is. Set up originally to flog off surplus server equipment from the Oracle company, this site has now become a market place for used Oracle software. Sadly, browsing this site is restricted to those who can register themselves as a business. Giving an idea of the site's global ambitions, it can also be read in Japanese, Chinese, Spanish, French and German.

Sci-quest Auctions   www.auctions-sciquest.com

US site for used and refurbished lab equipment from individual labs and manufacturers.

SeaNet   www.seanet.co.uk

Ships for sale, offers of transportation and tenders for goods to be shipped all meet up on this not especially wonderful site that still won a top site award from the *Financial Times*.

Southern Auctioneers   www.auctioneer.co.uk

'Assets disposal experts' Southern Auctioneers seem to be dipping their toe online with this site, where just a few pieces of industrial measuring equipment were for auction. Company boasts it can clear a whole factory anywhere in the world.

SteelScreen   www.steelscreen.com

Promising-looking European site for sale of steel. It was not fully up and running at the time of writing.

Sweeney-Kincaid   www.sweeney-kincaid.co.uk

Traditional real-time auction house that has gone tentatively online with auctions of heavy-duty construction and manufacturing equipment. At the time of writing the links were not all working, though the site claims to have completed its first online auction in

2000. This Glasgow-based company has links in the Middle East and Asia and specialises in bankrupt stock.

Trading Lounge www.tradinglounge.co.uk
The demand for fibre optic (the futuristic lights loved by groovy bars and restaurants) auctions here would appear to be justified by auctions from as far away as Hong Kong.

Ubid4it www.ubid4it.com
Small, bland US site with some 50 auctions for computer hardware and phones. Site offers escrow service.

UK Catering Auctions Online www.catering-auctions.co.uk
Promising-looking site still in its starting phase that aims to sell under the categories of cookers, fridges, freezers, ovens and other catering-related equipment.

World Internet Insolvency and www.insolvency.
Bankruptcy Resources com
Directory of links to insolvency auctions worldwide with a good page on the UK, where auctions of goods seized by bailiffs, customs and police feature. Mostly real-time auctions, though some of the UK links are branching out into online auctions.

//CARS AND NUMBER PLATES

Buying cars online has got underway on a big scale in the UK over the last few years, but the process of buying cars unseen has posed a big credibility problem. If the UK is to take the lead from the USA, the attraction for auctions would seem to lie in selling limited avail-ability classic cars, which would always attract a higher price when sold nationally rather than locally.

Autoseek www.autoseek.co.uk
UK site for car buyers with links to lots of humdrum-looking

real-time car auctions and at present one online auction. Worth checking out for new sites.

Autoweb   www.autoweb.com

Travelling across the USA and need to find a cheap car? This large established US site has a long list of cars from authorised dealers who each have to offer a 72-hour money-back guarantee and a three-month warranty. All cars are between one and four years old.

eBay Motors   www.ebaymotors.com

Great for a browse if nothing else, this site has all its photos automatically downloaded. There are some amazing classic cars for sale here such as E-type Jags and 1958 Cadillacs with tail fins. To get a better view, click on each photo for a close-up.

Ecarnut   www.ecarnut.com

A boon to UK classic car collectors, this site specialises in spare parts for classic Buick, Cadillac, Chevy, Ford, Hudson, Mercury and Oldsmobile cars. 1950s models dominate, though there are spare parts here from the 1920s–1960s. Speedometers, instrument panels, tail lenses, parking lamps and instrument clusters all feature heavily.

Exchange and Mart   www.exchangeandmart.co.uk

UK's long-running classifieds magazine has always been strong on classified adverts for cars. It has now gone online and offers its advertisers the chance to put their cars up for auction too, though it is early days yet with only 53 car-related auctions. Cars on offer range from a 1990 Fiat Panda with a new exhaust at £175 ($290) to a silver, C reg Mercedes 280SL in 'vgc' at £9,950 ($16,600). Unfortunately, at present there is no feedback rating system or bidding history. The only guarantees are that the site takes a 1-5% deposit from the winning bidder's credit card.

New Reg www.newreg.co.uk

This site offers a complicated-sounding procedure to obtain personalised UK car number plates at official auctions undertaken by 'experts'.

Personally Yours www.personallyyours.co.uk

A rather overpriced list of UK number plates, ranging from £500 ($830) to £12,000 ($20,000), for which this unsophisticated site accepts email bids. Some bidders have shown enterprise by offering lower than the going prices. The site will also bid on your behalf at number plate auctions and undertake number plate searches.

Swapman www.swapman.com

If you are holding your vintage Cadillac, Pontiac, Ford, Oldsmobile, Chevy, Buick, MAC or Dodge together with rubber bands and glue, you can now turn to this open, breezy site with over 1,000 lots of spare parts for mainly 60s cars.

Wonderful Auctions www.w-a.co.jp

The Japanese drive on the left-hand side of the road, which makes their second-hand cars popular in the UK. This site, which is in good English, has hundreds of cars waiting in Nagoya, Japan, to be shipped abroad, by boat or plane. Knowing the Japanese love of all things new, a lot of these cars are probably bargains. All cars are owned by the site, which prices everything in Japanese yen.

//CHARITIES

Charity auctions are a lovely concept in theory. The seller donates an unwanted item and names a charity to benefit from the proceeds of the sale. The buyer hopefully picks up a bargain and can feel good about spending their money.

In practice, though, a charity site needs lots of promotional publicity for it to attract buyers and sellers and, typically, some of the sites below suffer from low levels of activity. The successful sites listed seem to accept that there has to be a trade-off with those who donate to the site. This allows sellers to generate a little free publicity for themselves.

Most charity auctions are from the USA at the moment and the UK does not appear to have woken up to their potential. Charity auctions can also be found at eBay, Yahoo and QXL.

Afundraiser www.afundraiser.com

Auctions for US racing memorabilia, the proceeds of which go towards a bone marrow awareness action scheme.

Bids4kids www.bids4kids.com

Thirty thousand children in the USA suffer from cystic fibrosis; the proceeds of the occasional auctions on this site go towards the US Cystic Fibrosis Foundation.

Bluecycle www.bluecycle.com

A penny a pound from every sale on this site is donated towards UK crime-fighting by its organisers, the insurers CGU. The site covers an eBay-like range of items, with large computer and business-to-business sections. To tempt bidders, many high-profile items are regularly advertised in auctions starting at £1. Stock is a mixture of stolen items recovered from crime, salvaged and end-of-line items donated to the site. All payments go through an on-site escrow service.

Charity Auction www.charityauction.com

A worthy, professional site that allows you to sell items for the charity of your choice but at present only features a paltry ten auctions.

UK Fundraising   **www.fundraising.co.uk**

Excellent general site that often has links to some one-off charity auction, as well as a direct link to QXL's charity auction page.

WebCharity   **www.webcharity.com**

Successful US charity site that since starting in 1997 has sold 1,840 items and given $150,000 (£99,000) to charity; notable sales have been Courtney Love's guitar for $1,200 (£790) and a London double-decker bus at $18,000 (£12,000). All sellers who donate to the site can nominate any registered charity they choose.

//CLOTHING

Love That Look   **www.lovethatlook.com**

Lovely pastel-coloured wedding site with auctions from US dealers in bridal wear, under the categories of wedding gowns, accessories (gloves and jewellery), gifts, special occasion dresses, veils and head-dresses. Sadly, not all the photos were working when we looked.

Vintage USA   **www.vintageusa.com**

Nike Air Jordan trainers, or 'sneakers' as they call them in the USA, are the big items on this site that also has US military wear such as flying jackets and the obligatory vintage Levis. Holds around 100 auctions, with prices for sneakers ranging from $100 (£66) to $250 (£165).

//COINS

Coins are near perfect for trading at online auctions and generate a lot of sales. The coin auction world is full of nasty rumours that many dealers use online auctions to offload coins they have had trouble selling from their shops, but one site, Collectors USA, goes as far as to claim a policy against such practices. At present there are no UK online coin auctions, so there is a business opportunity out there for someone. Some of the biggest selections of coins are currently to be found at the general sites such as eBay, QXL and Yahoo.

Cce-Auction
www.cce-auction.com

Three thousand coins, but only 245 from 'the rest of the world'. Up-to-the-minute prices on gold, silver, platinum, rhodium and palladium can also be viewed here.

Collectors USA
www.collectorsusa.com

This site lambasts other coin sites that allow dealers to offload their 'ugly, problem' coins that are often over-graded and sold at 'bargain' prices. Collectors USA insists on higher standards from its dealers, who sell mostly US coins and medals here.

Currency Auction
www.currencyauction.com

From the same US company as Heritage Coin, this site specialises in vintage US bank notes, bonds and stocks. There were 314 lots here, with some interesting items such as Confederacy notes. All items are sold direct from the site.

Heritage Coin
www.heritagecoin.com

A big ugly site that grandly calls itself the world's largest numismatic dealer and auctioneer, yet stocks almost exclusively US coins and banknotes. Also a general resource for coin dealers with a 'What is my coin worth?' link and real-time auctions too. All coins sold are direct from the site, with a 15% buyer's fee.

Numis Media
www.numismedia.com

Professional but dull US site where registered dealers sell mainly US coins. Useful extras are an online price guide, news page, classifieds, dealer directory and bookstore.

Numismatists Online
www.numismatists.com

'The Internet's premier service for coin and currency collectors' apparently, which features occasional auctions from approved US dealers who sell mostly US coins, with a few ancient and world coin selections too. Each coin comes with a seven-day return 'privilege'. Also news, articles, book links and price guides.

//COMICS

Comic books thrive at auction sites and while there are large listings for comic auctions at both eBay and Yahoo, the following sites are worth checking out for their enthusiasm, knowledge and grading services.

The best

Comic Book Postal Auctions   **www.compalcomics.com**

This long-established UK company started out running postal auctions advertised in specialist magazines. Now on the Net, its online auction service has clocked up some notable sales, such as the first issues of *Spiderman*, *Daredevil*, *X-Men*, *Fantastic Four* and issues 6 and 7 of the *Beano* (which sold at £760/$1,260) each. There is a strong selection of classic British comics here too, such as *Hotspur*, *Eagle*, *Beezer*, *Victor*, *Wizzard*, *Dandy* and *Film Fun*. A drawback of the site is that you must still purchase the company's £7 ($12) catalogue before you can take part in the auctions, which are still run in conjunction with their old mail-order service. Bids can only be taken by email.

The rest

Comic Exchange   **www.comicexchange.net**

Disappointing US site whose corporate design is at odds with the artistry of the comics it sells. Despite an impressive range of Platinum, Gold, Silver and Modern Age comics and a fair selection of anime and manga cartoons, original artwork, toys and figurines, there is a very low bid rate for this site.

Mile High Comics   www.milehighcomics.com

Large US site offering *Marvel*, *Batman*, *Thor* and *Iron Man* at auctions hosted by the main Amazon auction site. Extras are an online store and further *Playboy*, Disneyania, *Star Trek* and Beanie Babies collectibles.

Vault Action Comics   www.vaultcomics.com

This London-based comic auction has a somewhat wobbly site at present, which features four one-off auctions a year. All comics are graded by the site, which handles all transactions and charges a 10% buyer's premium. At the most recent auction there was a good selection of British comics, such as *Victor*, *Buster*, *Lady Penelope*, *Tiger*, *Beezer* and *Dandy*, along with Gold, Silver and Bronze Age comics too.

//COMPUTERS

Computer products, in terms of value (if not volume), dominate online auctions. Nowhere else does the consumer face such a wide choice; even at sites like eBay, Yahoo and QXL you will find large listings. The following sites heavily feature merchant auctions of surplus and out-of-date stock and some also sell 'refurbished' stock, effectively second-hand equipment that has been serviced.

A warning: Beware of ridiculously low-priced MS software for sale. Microsoft, following its own research, found that 90% of the auctions advertising MS software turned out to be pirated copies. While cheap software may sound attractive, bear in mind that if someone is unscrupulous enough to sell it, they will have few qualms about ripping people off too. As a result, eBay has clamped down hard on this area of activity. Sega, Nintendo and Electric Arts have also reported similar scams.

The best

Deal Deal   www.dealdeal.com

The world's 30th largest online retailer, according to recent reports, which specialises in auctions of 'surplus, closeout and refurbished products' from JVC, Sony, Dell, Krups and Wilson. The emphasis is on electronic products with two large categories for general business equipment and computers. Each auction features a 'compare at' price, which is presumably (though the site does not say) the going retail price. Under business there were three packs of five Microsoft 'natural' keyboards at £108 ($179) each, with a compare at price of £323 ($489). NEC 15-inch colour monitors at £62 ($94) had a compare at price of £125 ($189). Shipping prices are also listed, along with a great mass of detail and good clear photos for most items. The site offers lots of customer support in terms of shipping, payment, technical support and advice on returned items.

Dell Auction   www.dellauction.co.uk

This tiny part of the Dell Corporation auctions off surplus Dell hardware in the UK. Some auctions are from individuals, though the official Dell Auctions have a guarantee of fast delivery and safer transactions. Auctions for desktops, workstations, printers, notebooks, servers, storage, accessories and monitors are all found here.

Haggle Online Auctions   www.haggle.com

Trading since 1996, Haggle has developed a strong online community of computer traders and features several thousand auctions in total, software making up the largest category. The site lists its top ten deals on its homepage, showing items such as a HP desk jet printer at $160 (£106) compared to a retail price of $249.99 (£165) and a digital camera at $171.99 (£113.50) compared to a retail price of $269.99 (£178). Auctions are a mix of merchant and C2C.

The rest

Aber Bid   www.aberbid.com
For people who know and love motherboards, CPUs, modems and video cards, this site is apparently targeted at 'the high performance computer upgrade community'. All goods are sold as new and direct from the site at discount prices.

Auction Laptops   www.auctionlaptops.com
'International winners welcome', entices this US site that has twenty laptops for auction. There is a healthy level of bidding here for attractively priced machines such as a second-hand Compaq LTE 5300 1.3GB/16MB at $99 (£65), which has a new retail value of $2,800 (£1,850). The site also sells new laptops at low prices and plans to branch out into desktop computers too.

Auction Mac   www.auctionmac.com
Just Apple Mac systems, hardware and software, but very few auctions at present.

Auction Watchers   www.auctionwatchers.com
This nifty and very simple site searches many of the top computer auctions online and tells you where the cheapest prices are on makes of computer hardware and software.

Bidnbuy Online Auctions   www.bidnbuy.com
Dublin-based merchant auctions of surplus computer products and peripherals will ship anywhere in Europe. Auctions are split into headings for boards, mass storage, memory, modems, multimedia, printers, processors, scanners and software, each item coming with a manufacturer's photo and description. There are

some low prices here such as a Windows 2000 set-up at £77 ($128), HP colour inkjet printers at £64 ($106) and Host Adaptor kits at £30 ($49).

Cnet   www.cnet.com

Enormous US computer portal that does not ship internationally for the time being but is of interest – especially if they change their shipping rules.

Elance   www.elance.com

Very original site that matches companies looking for jobs to be done by professionals with freelance specialists. The site covers all ranges of work but names web design as one of its most popular requests. Simply offer a competitive price and timescale for getting the job done and the company chooses from its bids.

It seller   www.itseller.co.uk

Helpful but characterless site that had 157 lots, ranging from computer hard drives and software systems to printers, mainly from merchants who often sell multiple items and charge VAT.

Microworld   www.microworld.co.uk

Software specialists in games and educational CD-ROMs, this grey and dour site has 300-plus auctions for items sold direct from the site. Despite its unsophisticated layout and bidding pages, this site attracts a fair amount of bidding. Add VAT to the winning bid price.

Morgan Auctions   www.morgan-auctions.co.uk

Upbeat, helpful and attractive, Morgan Auctions claims to have sold 10,000 items since starting in 1997. Often using a 24-hour auction format, it sells mainly end-of-line and bankrupt stock such as monitors, digital cameras and CD-ROM drives. Each is presented on the site with original supplier photos and lengthy descriptions. All lots come with UK shipping prices, supplier guarantees and are despatched within 48 hours. Add VAT to the price of all items on the site.

Outpost Auctions   www.outpostauctions.com

US merchant auctions for surplus computer equipment ranging from hardware upgrades to digital cameras and scanners, many starting from $1. Many of the auctions state that they will ship internationally.

Shopnow   www.shopnow.com

Some very good offers here for surplus and factory refurbished computers and laptops. For the US market only at present, but the site says it has plans to ship internationally.

//DANCE

Dance Auction   www.danceauction.com

Three hundred items of dance clothing, books, music, videos and accessories covering ballet, tap and ice skating at this US site. Also links, web rings and magazines.

//DECLINING AUCTIONS

Lets Buy It   www.letsbuyit.com

Lets Buy It is not an auction site as such, but it follows the same principles of bargain hunting mixed with uncertainty, which is typical of online auctions. Striking deals with up to 150 top brands, it offers their products for sale on its site. The deal is that the more people who register to buy a product, the lower the price becomes over a ten-day period. Upmarket electronics products such as digital cameras, DVD players and wide-screen TVs are typical of the site, which also branches out into areas such as cars and fashion. The site is easy to use, easy to understand and the delivery is free. Not surprisingly, Lets Buy It is already making a profit.

//DOMAIN NAMES

Never have so few earned so much from doing so little. The mindless business of plonking your flag on a domain name and then flogging it off to whoever is loaded or stupid enough to buy it has created a slightly unreal market in domain names. In a recent deal, business.com was sold for $7.5 million (£4.9 million). Maybe you will get a flicker of inspiration for your new Internet venture while browsing the list of domains on offer at the following sites. The best value from these sites, though, is looking at some of the ludicrous names and prices people are asking for. Domain auctions tend to have their own unique set of rules, not the least of which prevents you from claiming a name on which a brand name already exists.

The best

Great Domains   **www.greatdomains.com**

The biggest domain dealers, who not only auction, but also register, sell and lease domains. If your domain is a going concern, they can sell that too. They claim on last inspection to have 544,780 names for sale. The highest bid was $580,000 (£350,000) for digitalphone.com, though the site says it regularly takes transactions ranging from $500 (£330) to $1 million (£660,000).

The rest

Afternic   **www.afternic.com**

This helpful site lists 150,000 auctions and features an appraisal page to help find the likely value of your domain. Site categories run from adult to travel, though the business and entertainment categories were the largest. Notable bidding here included $9,000 (£6,000) for Madonnamusic.com and $600 (£400) for lovelymusic. com. No takers though for Ichewgum.com at $50 (£33).

Shout Loud www.shoutloud.com

Shout Loud bills itself as Europe's largest domain name exchange, but still it is mainly .com and .co.uk names for sale here among the 1,000 domains on offer, with all prices in dollars. The site gives some rather dopey details on each domain, for example, byyourhousehere.co.uk ($2,500/£1,650) is apparently suitable for house sellers and estate agents.

url merchant www.urlmerchant.com

A source of really lame domain names, prize turkeys being franceoui.com and russiasite.com. Fiend.com was more enticing but came at $75,000 (£49,000). The average price for sites here ranges between $5,000 (£3,300) and $15,000 (£9,900) with a minimum bid price of $750 (£500).

//ELECTRONICS

Audiogon www.audiogon.com

If you know the difference between an amplifier and a preamplifier then you will love this clear and concise US site for hi-tech music equipment. Its categories cover cables, digital, software, speakers and home theatre. Great manufacturers' links pages and discussion forums too.

Egghead www.egghead.com

Massive and professional US merchant auction that sells off consumer retail items in multiple lots direct from the site based in California. Using the Yankee auctions format, those with the largest quantity and highest bids are favoured. Its main categories are for computer products, sports and fitness, electronics and travel. There are bargains galore at this site, with many bids starting at $9 (£6), though not all products are open to international bids.

Sharper Image   **www.sharperimage.com**

There are daft gadgets to both amuse and amaze from this cool site based in San Francisco. Example offers include musical candles that, when lit, play 'Danny Boy' at $20 (£13), bagel slicers, a remote sensor for the weather outside your house, a turbo groomer for nose hairs and desktop dartboards. Most products come at tempting prices that show the markdown from their former retail price. The site accepts international orders and asks for credit card details upon registration.

//HOLIDAYS

Holiday auction sites at present seem a reliable source of bargains since, by their nature, they feature holidays that tour companies are finding hard to sell. On occasions they can provide some amazing offers, as Julie Humphreys of Bury found when, as a joke, she placed a 50p bid on a one-week holiday in Rhodes. Her bid was the only one received and so she was awarded the holiday and allowed to pay an extra 50p to take along her boyfriend too. UK Holiday auctions also mean that there has never been a better time for a weekend away; most auction sites are awash with bed and breakfast breaks at English seaside towns. For more holiday auctions also check http://auctions.excite.co.uk.

AdventureBid   **www.adventurebid.com**

Attractive US site selling adventure holidays such as kayaking, windsurfing, rafting, bear hunting and safaris.

Holiday Auctions   **www.holidayauctions.net**

Messy but popular site run by the Midlands Co-op Travel Agency, which says the site is the fifth largest holiday retailer in the UK. All holidays are listed by airport of departure from a choice of

Birmingham, Bristol, East Midlands, Gatwick, Glasgow, Luton, Manchester, Newcastle and Stansted. Top offers included seven nights self catering in Ibiza for 2–3 people at £100 ($166) from Gatwick, seven nights self catering in Fuerteventura for 2–3 people at £140 ($232) from Stansted and 7 nights self catering in Lanzarote for 2–3 people at £190 ($315) from East Midlands. Most deals had a departure date within 10–20 days.

iBidUSA   www.ibidusa.com

A unique holiday site devoted to Orlando, Florida, where everything from bed and breakfast to gift certificates for restaurants, bars, deep-sea fishing, the zoo and the Seaworld Center are up for auction. The registration form to the site, however, does not make a concession to those from outside the USA, which seems a little short sighted, but the site is worth a try anyway.

Last Minute   www.lastminute.com

Auctions are a new addition to the Last Minute site and at present feature a small mixed bag of flights, holidays and gifts. Their biggest attraction is British Midland flights to the UK and Europe, with deals such as return trips to Paris at £35 ($58) plus £24.90 ($41) airport taxes and a business-class return flight to Rome at £75 ($124) plus £23.50 ($39) tax and service. Also here are some one-off unusual and upmarket breaks, such as seven nights in a French château at £1,450 ($2,407) for two people, or £250 ($415) per person for a villa with its own pool in St Lucia. Beyond holidays, the site also hosts celebrity charity auctions, such as a signed photograph of the Rolling Stones and a Vivienne Westwood jacket. There is also a fully booked section offering tickets, where available, for sold out events.

Luxury Link   www.luxurylink.com

A private 'lodge' in a safari park, exclusive villas in palm-tree locations and suites in some of the most exclusive hotels in the world at bargain prices are all offered by tour companies as a promotional exercise at this site. Each advertises its real price alongside the auction starting price, so it is not surprising that the site also sells similar holidays at the going rate. Some of the holidays specify an opening flight from the USA.

Sky Auction www.skyauction.com
New York-based site that offers deals on flights and some holidays. Most flights start in the USA, although a few originate in London. United Airlines flights feature heavily.

Travel Break www.travelbreak.com
Large US site notable for its range of US hotel rooms; also travel news and message boards.

//HOLLYWOOD

If you are looking for more Hollywood or glamour star auctions, you will find many on general sites such as Firedup, QXL, Amazon and Goricardo, all which use them to generate publicity.

The best

Universal Studios Store www.universalstudios.com
Once you have got round some rather rusty links on this site, you will come across a treasure trove of movie memorabilia. Top stuff includes signed photos with some interesting bidding, for example, Jack Nicholson $105 (£69), Frank Sinatra $75 (£49), Pierce Brosnan $70 (£46) and Bruce Willis $55 (£36), with Keanu Reeves, Britney Spears and Mariah Carey down at $30 (£20). Also here is one of Cher's unwanted necklaces at $85 (£56), signed scripts from *Seinfeld*, *X-Files* and *ER*, plus old press packs, props and wardrobe items for top films. All items come with a certificate of authenticity and part of the winning bid goes towards charity.

The rest

The Broadcaster   www.thebroadcaster.com

Walk-on parts for shows such as *The X-Files* have been auditioned here. What you can normally expect are cast-signed movie/TV posters and scripts, plus VIP tickets to watch shows being made. All offers are donated to the site to fund the Broadcaster, a 'non profit organization to provide training opportunities to minority college graduates in radio/television news reporting and news management'. Top items spotted were a *Talented Mr Ripley* poster signed by Gwyneth Paltrow, Matt Damon and Jude Law with three bids at $300 (£200) and a poster from *NYPD Blue* signed by the cast at $150 (£100). The auction link is found on the bottom right of the Broadcaster's homepage.

Disney   www.disney.com

When we last looked, Disney – one of the top 10 biggest sites on the Net – were promising forthcoming auctions of 'Genuine memorabilia and treasures directly from Disney's timeless films, TV shows and theme parks'.

//JEWISH

Yehud   www.yehud.com

This Jewish portal site has a special auction link that searches Jewish-related auctions at eBay, Yahoo and Amazon under the categories of art, books, collectibles, Kiddush cups, Menorahs, Mezuzot and Passover Haggadot.

//LUXURY

You do not need to be a millionaire to browse the following sites, which, despite their image, are often not as expensive as they look.

Big Wig Auctions   www.bigwigauctions.com
Cars, collectibles, cigars, watches, wines and spirits. A very helpful
site, though no seller ratings for its mainly consumer-to-consumer
auctions.

Dupont Registry   www.dupontregistry.com
Evolved from a fifteen-year-old magazine aimed at the luxury
market, Dupont has done a good job with its site, turning it
into what looks like the market leader for luxury goods. Even if
you cannot afford anything here (though some cheap items do slip
through), it is still fascinating to see the photos, prices and
details for such items as a used Lear Jet starting at $1,585,000
(£1,046,100), a 1931 Rolls Royce at $178,000 (£117,500) or a 185-foot
US expedition yacht at $9,800,000 (£6,468,000). The full list of
categories is as follows: aircraft, antiques, art, autos, boats, cigars,
clothing, collectibles, electronics, executive gifts, furniture, golf,
gourmet food, jewellery, motorcycles, real estate, recreation, sports
memorabilia, travel and wines. Most auctions are C2C or, in this
case, millionaire to millionaire.

The rest

Bezign   www.bezign.com
A sleek soft-focus UK site aimed at parting rich women from
their money, Bezign features promotional one-off merchant
auctions for items at around a third of their retail price. Sample
items included a cashmere halterneck top, a blue crystal bracelet
set, diamond wristwatches and a sixteen-person ranch holiday
in Kenya.

Cyberhorse Online Auction   www.cyberhorseauction.com
A fascinating US site that auctions horses, each of which comes

with some refreshingly honest descriptions, for example, a twenty-year-old Arabian stallion will apparently 'weave if it is upset' but is still 'sound and sane', while a poor Shetland pony's owner says that it was kicked in the head and now has one cloudy eye.

Millionaire   www.millionaire.com

Occasional links to real-time auctions from US magazine *Millionaire*, of interest to the seriously rich.

Royalbid   www.royalbid.com

Fifty posh designer items for auction at lowish prices.

//MAKE-UP

If your make-up table is bulging with unused or unlikely-ever-to-be-used cosmetics, why not trade some of it online? That is the logic behind the following sites, which are also a reaction against some of the cheap marketing of cosmetics companies, so, as the Lipstick Page says, 'business owners not welcome'. At the following sites you are not just getting bargains, but also gaining the chance to swap make-up tips and chat. They also offer a more feminine alternative to some of the more macho competitive sides to online auctions. However, these sites employ the same principles of feedback ratings as normal auction sites.

Beauty Buzz   www.beautybuzz.com

'One girl's trash becomes another one's stash' is the curt tag line for this site, which is full of make-up tips, shopping pages, reviews and chat. The swapping here is not of the same volume as the above sites.

The Lipstick Page   www.thelipstickpage.com

'It's a beautiful fragrance, but it just didn't work for me' and 'Love the scent but my skin doesn't' are two of the reasons why women are putting ads here. Covering more than cosmetics, there are also haircare, bodycare and skincare products here. Register for swapping on this pink-coloured page and you will be given the title 'Junior'; a few successful swaps later and you can become a 'Senior' before progressing to becoming an 'Elite' member. A unique service, the 'Cosmetics Exchange Network' also lets you approach people who are able to buy cosmetics not available in your own location. Also a library and resource guide and a guide to the 'lipstick of the stars'.

Make Up Alley   **www.makeupalley.com**
Beautifully designed in pastel colours, this is the most popular of the make-up sites, carrying ads from both the USA and the UK. Lots come under headings for blushers, brushes, concealer, eyes, foundation, fragrances, mouth, nails and even a section for men too.

//MUSIC

There is, unfortunately, no one effective CD specialist auction site; if you are looking for CDs and records, your best bet is eBay. What you do have here, though, are some small sites catering for special markets.

The best

---

eRock   **www.erock.net**
This eBay-like operation fairly bills itself as 'The world's premier rock 'n' roll memorabilia auction site'. There were 1,463 items listed, with big categories for the Beatles, Elvis Presley, Kiss and the Rolling Stones. Much of the memorabilia is made up of magazines, stage passes, tickets, posters, 45s and LPs. Items of note were a 1976 Lou Reed backstage pass at $14.50 (£9.50) and a lovely repro poster for a Led Zeppelin gig at the Whiskey-a-go-go in LA with

Alice Cooper as support for $19.95 (£13). Also wanted pages, free image hosting, message boards and links.

The rest

All Jazz   www.alljazz.com

One-off monthly auctions of jazz 78s, LPs and some CDs. The huge 3,000 listing features large entries for Louis Armstrong and Cab Calloway. Based in New Jersey, All Jazz grades each record and sells direct from the site – email or fax bids are accepted.

CDSeek   www.cdseek.com

A great name and lots of categories but, rather like the *Marie Celeste*, this site was completely empty when we looked.

Dolphin Music   www.dolphinmusic.co.uk

Online retailers of hi-tech electronic musical instruments and equipment whose page devoted to auctions is slowly taking off.

Gibson Global Auctions   www.auction.gibson.com

Gibson owners send their guitars to the Gibson HQ in the USA, which then grades them and photographs them beautifully before posting them for auction. There were only fifteen auctions for guitars and amps but the site has the advantage of being able to authenticate each guitar, as there are reports of fake vintage guitars being sold to cater for demand. Sellers pay the auction site 10% commission and also pay for shipping. Main site has lovely photo gallery of Gibson guitars.

Good Rockin' Tonight   www.goodrockintonight.com

Single US dealer's collection of classic rock vinyl from the 1950s to the 1970s, as well as old blues 78s. The auction is hosted as part of a collective site of dealers called Collectors Universe. All records come with a 48-hour return privilege.

Guitar Auction   **www.guitarauction.com**

One hundred and fifty lots of used, new and vintage guitars and amps sold by guitar dealers and individuals in the US. A sophisticated site with a fair level of bidding.

Rare Soul Man   **www.raresoulman.co.uk**

One-off auctions for Northern Soul records on this obsessively compiled collectors' site.

Record Finders   **www.recordfinders.com**

There are thousands of 78s, LPs and 45s here, listed by long-established US newspaper *Record Finder*. Records from the 1940s–1960s dominate the collection. The site handles all payments and, lacking auction software, simply asks for you to send in your highest bid, by email presumably. The site also has fixed-price sales of vinyl and record players, message boards, a quiz and links.

Rock Auction   **www.rockauction.com**

This is a wonderful site that is, sadly, 'currently only shipping to the USA'. What you are missing out on is a collection of closeout, shop-damaged gear from top US music shops shipped to the warehouse of this site in New England. If you can put up with a few scratches, you can get Marshall practice amps from $55 (£36) and less famous ones at $35 (£23). Other prices included Epiphone guitars at $175 (£115) with a retail price of $499 (£329).

//POKEMON

The best Pokémon listings are to be found on eBay, Yahoo and the like, though the US Pokémon Nation at **www.collectingnation.com** is of interest, with several thousand Pokémon auctions and links on its site.

//PROPERTY

Selling your house works pretty much in the same way as an auction in that the highest bid usually wins.

Allsop www.auction.co.uk

The main site of Allsop & Co, which bills itself as the biggest auctioneer of property in Europe. All property is sold through real-time auctions but this site accepts email bids and shows its catalogue online.

Easier www.easier.co.uk

A new and totally free UK service for those looking to buy or sell homes. The deal for the site is that your details are passed on to surveyors and solicitors necessary for the completion of property deals. A fair exchange, maybe, for not having to deal with any more estate agents. Not a great deal of property yet, but this looks promising.

Nerex www.propertyfind.co.uk

This small grey site searches for homes for sale by UK county and price range. If you like what you see then you can email the owner directly.

Property For Auction www.propertyforauction.co.uk

Buyers register here and leave details of the properties they are looking for and the price ranges they can afford. The site then emails them details as and when they become available. For sellers, a listing with one photo costs £9.99 ($16) and a listing with three photos costs £75 ($124); for £99 you get a sale board and for £199 they will manage all enquiries too. The site also links you to companies such as property surveyors.

//REVERSE AUCTIONS

Reverse auctions can provide a well-earned holiday for dedicated buyers at online auctions. In a reversal of conventional auctions it is the buyers who post the adverts to the site, in which they describe exactly what it is they are after and the sort of price they are prepared to pay. The buyer then puts their feet up and waits for the offers to come rolling in. The buyer is free to choose the best offer received.

The reverse auction sites listed below come with their own sets of rules. One of their features is that they will often be in contact with suppliers, to whom they forward many of the buyers' adverts on this site. Any reverse auctions of any merit will promise a no-spam policy and for the buyer there is also the attractive benefit that they do not have to leave their credit details with the site.

To what extent reverse auctions will catch on in the UK remains to be seen. At present there is no notable reverse auction site specifically catering for the UK. Meanwhile, three of the biggest reverse auction sites, **imandi.com**, **respond.com** and **priceline. com**, unfortunately only accept registration from people with a US or Canadian zip code and therefore have not been listed below.

The best

ewanted   www.ewanted.com

Ewanted has taken off in an eBay-style in the USA, with its unique service that enables buyers to seek out items not normally found in shops. Typically these are items that are out of production or perhaps missing parts of machines, so it is hardly surprising to find that the largest category is for automobile parts. One of the site's biggest attractions is that you might find that some of the junk you have lying around at the back of your cupboard is actually something that somebody wants to pay you hard cash for. Some of the more bizarre ads on the site were for seafood at $2 a pound and an offer to send in unopened bubble gum packets from around the world. The site, although based in the USA, features adverts from around the world.

The rest

Bidders Paradise   www.biddersparadise.com
Straightforward but dull US reverse auction site aimed at matching consumer buyers to business sellers. The site accepts international registration.

Reverse Auction   www.reverseauction.com
Not happy sticking to one auction gimmick with its reverse auctions, this large US site also went and created another, the declining auction. This novelty auction works by sellers listing an advert at its maximum price. Over the seven days of an auction, a computer at the site chips a cent off every so often, so as the week progresses the price gets lower and lower until at the end of the week it hits the absolute minimum the seller would want to sell for. Buyers can nip in to buy whenever they see the price they like. In a variation on the autobid mechanism, buyers can register a price they are prepared to pay with the site and when the price falls to that level and the item has not sold, they win. This site accepts registration worldwide.

Reverse Bids   www.reversebids.co.uk
Small UK site suffering from a lack of publicity that at present has only a few adverts.

//SCIENCE

Science auctions are not exactly setting the auction world alight, but all the following seem very worthy.

Chem Exchange   www.chemexchange.com

Chemicals such as Efka 401 Polymer and BASF Laromer HDDA on offer at prices as low as $1. Also chemical-processing equipment.

Doction   www.doction.com

Soon-to-be-launched auctions for and by the medical community.

Planet Test   www.planettest.com

Meters, oscilloscopes, testers, analysers and invertors all being auctioned off at low prices by US merchants.

TestBid   www.testbid.com

Test and measurement equipment for auction at this US site with only two items at the last time of looking.

//SEWING

Cross Stitches Auction   www.xstitches.com

A neat and popular auction page notable for its large number of old sewing patterns but also featuring sewing magazines, books, fabric, sewing kits, needlepoint and canvas.

//SPORTS

Golf

The best

Golf Club Exchange   www.golfclubexchange.com

A site that just auctions golf clubs might seem a poor business venture, but Golf Club Exchange did $3 million (£2 million) worth of business in 1999. This is due partly to a winning mix of simplicity and efficiency in the site design, which simply requires the buyer to select a category from sets, irons, woods, wedges or putters, choose a size or brand and then browse the results. Extras are an onsite escrow system, a price guide, a shop and golf-related links. It is reassuring to note that many sellers have high feedback ratings.

Golf Store   **www.golfstore.co.uk**

There must be some connection between liking golf and being good at websites because this is another gem of a site, being easy to use and attractively laid out. To enter, first choose the auctions link from the home shopping site; here you can browse categories for sets, irons, woods, putters, wedges, bags and more. These categories contained only eleven auctions, but there was a high level of bidding on most.

The rest

Easy Golf   **www.easygolf.co.uk**

A dull site with a big online shopping catalogue for golfers and an auction page that announces 'A fully comprehensive auction site will be here soon'. Perhaps it's now up and running.

FishGolf   **www.fishgolf.com**

Fishing reels, rods and accessories are in the top half of this US site and golf irons, sets and accessories sit in the bottom.

Soccer

Soccer auctions have great potential in the UK, but sites such as QXL and eBay have taken most of this up. The dull, conservative corporate stance of most UK football club sites seems largely to blame. At the time of writing, the following were the only premiership clubs holding or mentioning auctions on their sites.

Chelsea FC   www.chelseafc.co.uk

A football shirt signed by the current Chelsea squad and a historic photo of the 1970 team holding the FA Cup were the only items listed here. As the links to the bidding pages were not working, it seemed to suggest that these auctions had long finished. If you're looking for the auction page at this site, try doing a search on the word 'auction' from the homepage.

Leeds United FC   www.lufc.co.uk

No auctions here, despite them being mentioned on the shopping page banner – perhaps this is in the pipeline.

Sunderland AFC   www.sunderlandafc.co.uk

Auctions can be found here under the shopping page, but you are only allowed to browse if you register first.

General

Coubertin   www.coubertin.com

Unlikely but intriguing Olympic site whose main claim to fame is the auctioning of medals. Real winners' medals are few and far between and the best on offer was a silver medal from the 1956 winter games, though there were fourteen Olympic participation medals (one going back as far as the 1906 games in Athens) at prices between $200 (£132) and $300 (£200). Despite the dollar values this site is based in England and also auctions posters, tickets, coins, stamps, postcards, videos and books.

eSportstuff   www.esportstuff.com

US sports cards and autographs.

Live To Play   www.livetoplay.com

US merchant auction offering surplus stock bargains in outdoor sports and activity gear. Each auction tempts you with the former retail or 'compare' price; for example, a small snow tent going at $72 (£47) was compared to a 'suggested retail price' of $190 (£125). All transactions are with the site, which also offers a returns policy.

Mountain Zone   www.mountainzone.com

Anything mountain and snow related, from skis and hiking to climbing gear and snowboarding, is catered for on this large merchant auction site with shopping and news pages.

Rotman Auction   www.rotmanauction.com

Odd name, but great site for US sports memorabilia fanatics. Features real-time auctions for cards, autographed photos, bats, balls and books. Many items date from the 1940s to the 1960s and they cover the sports of baseball, basketball, boxing, American football, golf, hockey and racing. Online bids are accepted and winners are charged a 10% buyer's premium.

Rugby Rugby   www.rugbyrugby.com

Brilliant rugby news and shopping site that, for some reason, is based in Birmingham, Alabama, yet reports on European, South African, Australian and New Zealand rugby. Holds occasional auctions of rugby memorabilia.

Sporting Auction   www.sportingauction.com

Bargains galore at this surplus merchant auction of sports gear and adventure activity wear. Each item has listed both its auction price and its former retail price; for example, a stingray paintball gun for auction at $37 (£24) would normally sell at $89.99 (£60). All products come with good photos, long descriptions and shipping prices, though some face an export restriction. The site categories cover everything from skateboarding and skiing to soccer and cycling. All transactions are direct with the site.

Tennis Interactive   **www.tennisinteractive.net**
This British tennis news and shopping service site recently held one-off auctions for Wimbledon umpires' chairs and centre court nets.

//STAMPS

Stamp collectors, so often the butt of jokes, are having the last laugh with online auctions. No item is better suited to worldwide trading online than stamps because of the negligible shipping costs. Indeed, many US sites charge nothing for postage within the USA, going up to a paltry $1 for sending internationally. Stamps feature heavily at all the big general sites, but the following businesses offer more in terms of grading services and overall knowledge of the sector.

The best

Sandafayre Online   **www.sandafayre.com**
Even Americans seem to acknowledge this Manchester-based company as being the number one stamp auction site. Trading in stamps for a quarter of a century, Sandafayre had a turnover of $25 million (£16.5 million) in 1999. The company operates by buying up stamps from private collectors for which they pay anything between £100 ($166) and £5,000 ($8,300). All stamps are then graded and sold on direct to the public, who are charged an extra 14% buyer's premium but get a seven-day approval period in return. The site allows you to search by country or theme and features an impressive gallery page of stamps from around the world to whet your appetite. The site also offers news, articles and books.

Wardrop's Philately Online   www.wardrop.co.uk

If the 14% buyer's premium at Sandafayre is a turn-off, this excellent site has compiled a links page of dealers' stamp auctions from as far off as Israel, Scandinavia, New Zealand and the USA. These sites range from the woefully amateurish to the professional to eBay stamp auctions. Also links to clubs, societies and collectors, plus philatelic software, insurance for collectors and forum pages.

The rest

Award Masters Philatelics Online   www.awardmasters.com

Small site of around 200 lots which, unusually for an American site, has a good range of stamps from around the world.

Philatelists Online   www.philatelists.com

Yet another US site with an over-inflated image, billing itself as 'The Internet's premier service for stamp collectors'. Actually features some rather dull collections from professional dealers of mostly US or Canadian stamps. All stamps come with a seven-day return agreement.

Stanley Gibbons   www.stanleygibbons.com

Despite being 'by appointment to Her Majesty the Queen', Stanley Gibbons has lost much ground to Sandafayre. Opting for quality rather than quantity, it holds a handful of multiple-lot auctions each month. The four being held in June 2000 were postcards (39 lots), stamps (1,111), stamps with errors (78) and first-day covers (64), each lot coming expertly photographed and graded. All transactions take place with the site, which charges a buyer's fee and also warns that in some cases VAT may be charged. There are also shops, magazines and books for sale here.

//STRANGE SITES

Weirdo websites proliferate on the Net and the world of online auctions is not without its fair share.

247guns   www.247guns.com

Rather than being the proud, conservative, upfront site banging on about its right to bear arms, which is what one might expect here, this actually turns out to be a primitive message board for those looking to buy and sell handguns, rifles and knives, plus a category called 'Whatever you have lying around', which includes hunting clubs. The star sale here was for an AK-47, with a case of 'ammo' thrown in, at $995 (£657). Needless to say, you cannot legally import the guns to the UK.

Meta Exchange   www.metaexchange.com

Beanie Bear mania reaches its nadir at this site which charts the rise and fall of Beanie prices at auction in the USA as if they were listed on the stock exchange. Each bear is assigned its own 'trading pit' at which there is shown a three-month price index for the value of that bear. Submit a bid price to the site, which will then try to match you with someone who will sell at this price. The top seller was the pink Sakura bear at $84 (£55).

Auction Adventures   www.auctionadventures.net

Small and weird general US site from the Midwest with requisite black pages and some truly bizarre auction category headings such as Wheaties boxes. Under some of the more innocuous headings, items range from the sinister – a Nazi flag at $7.24 (£4.78) – through the inane – personalised Christmas bulbs – to the political – anti-Bill Clinton mouse pads at $3 (£2) that say 'Bill doesn't inhale, he just sucks'. Worth a browse.

Meteorites Inc   **www.meteorites.com**

Martian rock found in Los Angeles in 1931 and pieces of other meteorites that have landed on the USA are collected at this home site of a meteorite buff. You can browse at this site, but click on a rock to bid and you are taken through to eBay, where Meteorites Inc had a recent feedback rating of 182.

//TICKETS

The sale of tickets for sold-out events is one of the great opportunities thrown up by online auctions. However, at present in the UK there is great resistance to the idea, since it is usually associated with the barely legal practice of ticket touting. In June 2000 there were reports of numerous Euro 2000 tickets for sale at QXL, which was then forced to remove them after protests by the tournament's organisers. Their reasoning was that as each ticket had the name of the original purchaser printed on it, the organisers held the right to refuse entry to anyone whose name did not match that on the ticket. In practice such checks probably rarely happen and such a risk might be worth taking. Where there is a will there is a way and it looks likely that buying tickets for sold-out events, at higher than the outlet price, will become common through online auctions. While QXL pulled their Euro 2000 tickets auction, there were still more available at eBay. See also **www.lastminute.com** for other sold-out events tickets.

All Sold Out   **www.allsoldout.com**

A sign of how big ticket sales could become in the UK, this site has some 35,000 tickets available for US rock concerts, sports events and theatre shows. This could be useful if you are travelling to the USA and it is also interesting to see acts touring that rarely make it to the UK, such as Bruce Springsteen playing at the MGM Grand

Hotel in Las Vegas. All Sold Out also has tickets for the occasional European event, such as Euro 2000 and the French Tennis Open.

First Call Tickets   **www.firstcalltickets.com**
Primarily a site for the sale of fixed-price tickets, this large site also auctions tickets for a tame selection of mainstream pop shows and holidays. The travel auctions page turned out to be empty, but under pop there were lots of tickets for acts such as Tina Turner, Elton John, Britney Spears and Gabrielle. All tickets come as pairs and generally start out lower than the market price. It is not clear whether these were ruses designed to shift tickets for poor-selling shows or if any of the tickets featured were for sell-out shows. There is a £1.50 ($2.50) handling charge for each set of tickets.

Tickets   **www.tickets.com**
US tickets site much smaller in scale than All Sold Out, with tickets for sports events and music and theatre shows.

//TOYS

If you are looking for toys of relevance for today's kids, your best bet is eBay, QXL and Yahoo. Some of the following sites do also stock up-to-date toys, but they cater more for collectors seeking out such gems as those 1960s matchbox James Bond Aston Martins with spikes that shoot out the back.

The best

---

eHobbies   **www.ehobbies.com**
Ambitious site that offers a whole online community for toy collectors with magazines, shops, contests and chat rooms. Its busy auction categories feature around 500 lots of model trains, radio-controlled toys, die-cast toys (mostly cars), rocketry, tools and

supplies and models. Furthermore, its auction help pages are among the most helpful of any auction site.

Vectis   www.vectis.co.uk

Lovely UK site for vintage toys that are sold in real-time auctions, that accepts online bids. The site inspects each toy and applies its own grading system, provides detailed descriptions and then professionally photographs them. After the auction, Vectis processes all transactions and pays for shipping, in return for a 15% buyer's premium and a 2% credit card charge where used. The bi-monthly auctions are large in size, the last featuring 726 Dinky toys and 612 Corgi toys and a separate auction of model trains. The site also offers online shopping and a database of past auctions for price comparisons.

The rest

Buz & Norma Ray/BDA Auction   www.buznorma.com

Large one-off auctions every few months of Lionel toy trains from this site based in Michigan.

Collector Auctions   www.collectorauctions.com

Mostly Lionel toy trains from 1901 to the present day on this US site.

Magic Auction   www.magicauction.com

A fascinating, if badly designed, site for professional magicians. Its auction rules are unclear, though from what can be deduced it holds an auction every week covering anything from magic videos to stage platforms, books, coffins, chambers, lighting, sound systems and escape accessories and so on. For non-magicians the site is of interest in that by selling many of their props, the magicians have to reveal how their illusions work; for example, one advert baldly states that a pair of hand and leg cuffs is 'gimmicked for quick release'. The site seems to hold all items and pass them on in an escrow-like operation.

Mobilia   www.mobilia.com

Just toy cars here and, from 2,000 auctions, the healthiest trade was in Hot Wheels, with accessories, parts and restoration supplies and services. Some Matchbox models were also on offer. Useful extras are a news page, a price guide, shopping links and classifieds.

Rail Collectibles Online   www.aviation-show.com

Like a disused railway line, there is not much activity on this well-meaning site for model trains, but possibly worth a look.

Theriaults   www.theriaults.com

Theriaults runs real-time auctions of antique and collectible dolls all over the USA and auctions a few extra online at this site. Judging by the quality on offer here, the best stuff goes in the live auctions and these are the dolls they cannot sell elsewhere. The site offers doll appraisals, news and teddy bears too.

Thunder Bid   www.thunderbid.com

Hundreds of auctions from US dealers for mostly toy trains and some 'vintage toys'.

Wallis & Wallis   www.wallisandwallis.co.uk

Glib, unhelpful site that has links to monthly real-time auctions of militaria and vintage toys held in Lewes, East Sussex. Bids are accepted by email.

//WINES

When it comes to online auctions, wine is best left to the expert sites. eBay does not allow any sort of alcohol to be auctioned on its site and, while Yahoo has a reasonable listing, there is none of the confidence in bidding there that you will find at the best sites below. Watch out when buying wine abroad as the customs duty might make it prohibitively expensive.

The best

WineBid
www.winebid.com

Running since 1996, this site has built up a big reputation due to its founder David Elswood having invented wine auctions at Christies as far back as 1966. The site splits its auctions into UK, US and Australian locations. Its UK operation, which kicked off in 2000, is already doing good business with one large auction held every month. All purchases are charged 12.5% by the site, which handles all transactions.

The rest

Auction Vine
www.auctionvine.com

San Francisco-based site formerly linked to top US wine auctioneers Morrell & Co, which boasts that it once sold a 1870 Château Lafite Rothschild at $12,650 (£8,350). At the time of writing it had 150 auctions, largely from professional wine dealers. Naturally, considering its location, this site is strong on Californian wines.

Brentwood Wine Company
www.brentwoodwine.com

Specialists in one-off sales of vintage wines, this US site was selling 'the oldest known German wine in existence' (dating from 1727) with a bid at $2,600 (£1,716). All transactions are with the site, which charges a 12% buyer's premium.

Jordan & Jordan
www.saarwein.com

This German site for wines from the Saar looks promising but had a zero next to all its auction categories at the time of writing. Prices are in Deutschmarks, though the actual auction pages come in English and German.

Magnum Wines www.magnumwines.com
One-off auctions of enormous consignments of wine. At the last auction prices ranged from $1,300 (£858) for a 1961 bottle of Château Latour to $275 (£181) for six bottles of 1984 Napa Valley Merlot. Transactions are made to the site and come with a 10% charge.

Save The Grapes www.savethegrapes.com
Nice looking C2C site with a silly name and only twenty lots, showing that in this line of business it pays to stick to the more traditional sites like WineBid.

UK Universal Wine Exchange www.uvine.com
Ambitious, new and glossy-looking wine site run by an ex-head of Christies auctions is due to start trading soon.

Wine Commune www.winecommune.com
US C2C site strong on Californian wines. Notable wines included an 1898 Château Latour and a Jeroboam of Mouton Rothschild 1982 at $2,210 (£1,460).

8//TRIVIA

Famous auctions

1 A dinner date with Bill Cosby, the proceeds of which were given to charity.

2 Courtesy of the *Sun* newspaper, Firedup.com offered a dinner date with a Page 3 girl.

3 One of the 25 surviving original copies of the 1776 US Act of Independence sold at Sothebys.com for £5 million ($8.3 million).

4 A Californian lawyer who sold his garage junk on eBay got £88,591 (about $147,000) for a painting he bought at a jumble sale many years ago. His wife insisted he kept it in the garage.

5 A unique tape of a Paul Simon performance in England during the 1960s, which included a song never previously released by him, was auctioned at eBay.co.uk.

6 QXL won the contract to sell off Wembley stadium as it was being dismantled, its most popular items being pieces of the famous Wembley turf.

7 Margaret Thatcher's handbag, an iconic memento from her years in power, was auctioned at eBay.co.uk, the proceeds going to charity.

8 A walk-on part in a TV show, auctioned by Firedup.

9 A New York delicatessen at $190,000 on eBay.com.

10 The winning Chelsea Flower Gardens Show 2000 at eBay.co.uk.

Ten notorious auctions

1 A baby auctioned by its parents in Chicago. Auction removed by eBay.

2 A human kidney reached a value of $5,750,100 (about £3.8 million) before the auction was removed by eBay.

3 Twenty-nine year-old Kembrew McLeod made $1,325 (£875) for selling his 'immortal soul' after ten days' bidding at eBay. The winner received a jar labelled 'Kembrew's soul' with a certificate of ownership, some stickers and little plastic totems.

4 Mike Tyson's stolen 1986 WBA and WBC championship belts. The auction reserve price was not met and the seller was apprehended weeks later.

5 Five front-row tickets at $100 each to see the execution of Michael Toney, convicted of murdering three people in Forth Worth, Texas. Auction removed by eBay.

6 Four high school students in New Jersey vomited and became disorientated after allegedly buying the drug dextromethorphane at eBay.

7 A human skull brought back from the Korean War. Auction stopped by eBay.

8 The French government took Yahoo Auctions to court over what it claimed were over 1,000 items of Nazi memorabilia on its site including coins, flags and pictures.

9 Ubid caused controversy recently by reneging on some auctions for computerware that had been won at low prices. The site backed up the merchant who had created the auction; the merchant claimed that he had placed them there by

mistake. Yet this mistake was not noticed until after the auction had been completed.

10 Proof that almost anything will sell was established when a dealer at eBay.com sold the detritus that he'd found stuck down the bottom of his sofa for $7.

Top ten most popular auction items

1 Beanies
2 Pokémon
3 US sports cards
4 Computer software
5 Computer hardware
6 CDs
7 LPs
8 Stamps
9 Books
10 Jewellery

Top ten best sites just to browse

1 www.dupontregistry.com
2 www.ebaymotors.com
3 www.ebaygreatcollections.com
4 www.gavelnet.com
5 http:/sothebys.amazon.com
6 www.ukiyo-e-world.com
7 www.ewanted.com
8 www.sothebys.com
9 www.ebay.com
10 www.firedup.com

//GLOSSARY

autobid You, as the bidder, set the highest figure you would want to pay on the bidding form yet start bidding from a lower figure. If anyone bids above your starting figure, the site bids on your behalf up to the point when your highest figure is reached.

bidder The prospective buyer, who places a bid or offer of money on to an auction item.

B2B Business-to-business auctions.

B2C Business-to-consumer auctions.

C2C Consumer-to-consumer auctions.

deadbeat bidder A buyer who fails to honour their side of the deal after they have won an auction.

Dutch auction An auction lot with multiples of the same item, from which there can be several winners.

English auction A standard auction.

escrow A payment service offered by companies such as I-escrow.com, which acts as a third party adjudicator in a transaction, ensuring the seller gets paid and the buyer gets the goods.

maximum bid See autobid.

proxy bid Same as autobid.

real-time auction Basically an old-fashioned auction in a big hall, where the items and (most of) the bidders are physically present and where someone bangs a gavel at the auction's close.

reverse auction Where the buyer places the advert and the sellers make the bids.

shilling A conniving seller assumes another identity to place bids on their own auction in order to boost the price up.

sniping Unpopular process whereby someone who previously has had no involvement in an auction places a winning bid on an item in the dying seconds.

//WEBSITE INDEX

//INDEX

Also published in the Virgin Internet Guide series...

The Virgin Guide to the Internet
The advice you need to plug in, log on and get going.

The Virgin Family Internet Guide
The only book that lets your family get the best out of the Internet
– and lock out the worst.

The Virgin Internet Shopping Guide
You can now buy almost anything on the Internet, and this book
shows you how.

The Virgin Internet Travel Guide
The complete guide to choosing your destination
– and getting the best deal online.

The Virgin Internet Money Guide
Get your personal finances sorted – online.

The Virgin Internet Music Guide
The web is alive – with the sound of music.

The Virgin Internet Business Guide
The essential companion for anyone in business.

The Virgin Internet Research Guide
How to find just about anything on the Net.

Coming soon:

The Virgin Weird Internet Guide
Strange and wonderful places to surf.

The Virgin Internet Guide for Kids
Especially for the youngsters.

For more information, ask your friendly local bookseller -- or check
out our website: **http://www.virginbooks.com**